War, Sacrifice and Returning Home: A Compilation

Editor/Author
John R. Ostwald

Cover Design : Slate Run Publishing, LLC
Published by Slate Run Publishing LLC.
www.slaterunpub.com

ISBN-13: 978-0-692-84389-5

For all veterans, past, present and future.

"War is an ugly thing, but it is not the ugliest of things. The decayed and degraded state of moral and patriotic feeling which thinks that nothing is worth war is much worse. A man who has nothing for which he is willing to fight, nothing he cares about more than his own personal safety, is a miserable creature who has no chance of being free, unless made so by the exertions of better men than himself."

—John Stuart Mill

Honor the Warrior not the war.

—IVAW

Some Gave All

—B.R. Cyrus

The editor would like to thank the following for their kind contributions to the photo gallery:

Stephen Ross, Ashley Gallager, Stephen Onley, Robert Porter, Kristin Laplante, Kyra Te Paske, Christopher Meyer, John Holmes, Chris Antal, Ashley Gallager, Judith B. Valenti, Kath Dean, Frank Desorbo, Kevin Murphy, Steven Keuhn, Patrick Russo, Michael Coca, Ann Marie Lavoie, Brother Ken Lucas, Chris Casanova, Christine Rem, Chris Meyeer, Anthony Pascarella, Sr.

As a veteran and child of vets, as journalist, writer, educator and activist, John Ostwald has been a fierce advocate for our veterans and everything we need to know about them. A Troy native, John has spent his life recording the important events and people of our region. In this collection from his newspaper columns over the decades, John turns his heart and eyes on the full range of issues facing our veterans - from honoring his World War II vet mother to representing challenged veterans in our courts - and everything in between. John's columns help us appreciate the love, devotion and service of our veterans, and also the unique challenges they face in society.

Read John's book as an education and revelation into the hidden yet honored and precious lives of the veterans among us.

Edward Tick, Ph.D.
Director, Soldier's Heart
Author: *War and the Soul* and *Warrior's Return*

Contents

1. I LOOK FORWARD TO MEETING HIM 31
2. PATRIOT FLIGHT: TRIP OF HONOR FOR THE GREATEST GENERATION 35
3. HELPING HIM TELL HIS STORY 39
4. CARING MEANS SHARING THE BURDEN.. 43
5. EXCITEMENT, APPREHENSION AHEAD.... 47
6. HEALING THE WOUNDS OF WAR 51
7. DISCOVERING PEACE AND HEALING........ 55
8. TRIP TO VIET NAM DEEPLY MOVING 59
9. WELCOME AND THANKS 63
10. BROTHER KEN IS A HERO OF LIFE 67
11. THOUGHTS OF 911 AND IRAQ 71
12. A LETTER FROM IRAQ 75
13. THE SENTENCING OF A MARINE 79
14. STUDENT VETERANS NEED OUR SUPPORT 83
15. WAR HEALING CIRCLES........ 87
16. WHEN A CHAPLAIN DIES IN WAR........ 91
17. EVENTS THAT SUPPORT OUR VETS MEMORIAL DAY WEEKEND 2013........ 95
18. WHAT'S REALLY IMPORTANT? 99
19. VETERANS NEED MORE THAN PRAISE .. 103
20. ONE NEVER GETS OVER A BIG LOSS....... 107
21. VETERANS PART I 111
22. I'M PROUD TO BE AN AMERICAN 115
23. BOOT CAMP MEMORIES 119
24. KOREA:THE FORGOTTEN WAR 123

25. A DRY POST 127
26. VETERAN'S JUSTICE 131
27. WHO ARE VETS - THEY ALL TOUCH OUR LIVES 135
28. A SERVICEMAN'S FIRST VETERAN'S DAY – DON'T JUST THANK; BE THANKFUL 139
29. MORAL DILEMMAS..............................144
THE BEST JOB I EVER HAD 168
THEM 172
THE COMBAT VETERAN AT HOME.................. 176

Editor's Introduction

This is a simple book of reverence and remembrance. It is about the men and women who served during wartime and peacetime. It is about families and neighbors whose prayers guided them while they were far from home. It is a book that wasn't planned. Most of it is the result of my intermittent writing, on a variety of topics, over the last twelve years in two local newspapers. Most often for The Record based in Troy, New York then a few years later in the Saratogian. The columns about the armed forces flowed easily because it is very much apart my world and a very intimate part of all of our lives. It helped that my mother, age ninety, and dad, who is deceased, were both in the army. Their service gave me lots of material. The tragic death of my uncle, a young marine, also provided some additional passion. Finally, my own service during the Viet Nam era helped to provide some perspective.

When my colleagues and I met to do the initial planning for the book, it was clear that trying to focus on one aspect of the armed forces experience would be difficult. My columns mention a host of topics including a journey to Viet Nam for reconciliation and healing, trips to the war memorials in Washington D.C., boot camp experiences, the death of a chaplain, PTSD, a War Healing Circle for younger vets and many other topics but still there were many topics untouched. After much discussion we decided on a potpourri of sorts. This book contains not only my columns but meaningful photographs and additional heartfelt stories of sacrifice written by veteran friends. Our hope is that the words and images in the book promote more understanding of time in service but also the salient challenges of return to civilian life.

Publisher's Note

The question of the extent of change wrought upon the human personality, perhaps the essential nature of the individual her or himself, by service in the United States military is profound and unanswerable. Some most certainly find their true calling in the Army, Air Force, Navy, Marines, National Guard or Coast Guard. Some find themselves immersed in a culture neither to their liking nor to their sense of human purpose. Some serve, return to civilian life, and forge ahead without looking back. Others, a distinct minority I speculate, find themselves forever altered, perhaps by a lifetime career dedicated to an heroic ideal, perhaps simply by the proximity of life's inextricable entanglement with death. Others, whether career soldiers or short timers, war veterans or peacetime soldiers, as a result of immersion in a culture of clearly defined and transcendent values, objectives, and responsibilities, return to the world with a light which has been kindled within them and with an undeniable need to share that illumination with others.

As publisher of this piece, I offer brief sketches of five lives such as these last and one further of a woman, a former student of mine, currently serving in the Air

National Guard. I am confident that her light already shines and that it will grow even brighter as time flows by. These are special people, products of many sources other than the military yet stamped with the sign by which one recognizes the veteran of honorable service. Not all, but undoubtedly much, of who they were and are is due to their terms of service, their times of spiritual as well as physical and psychological transformation within the armed forces of the United States of America.

The chronological scope of the written component of this book extends from World War II up to and including Iraq and Afghanistan. My character sketches should serve as a taste of that which is to follow. Mr. Ostwald's newspaper columns and the selected photographs from his own library, some of which precede WWII, the recent images of Stephen Kuehn's, and the various contributions of so many others complete a complex panorama of those veterans who have lived among us and those who continue to grace our reality with their presence.

A commonly heard expression these days is, "Thank you for your service." Many veterans appreciate the sentiment. Others do not. This offering is not of such nature. It is neither an expression of gratitude nor an anthem to heroic military glory. The Marine Corps has a slogan: THE FEW. THE PROUD. THE MARINES. In the immediate aftermath of WWII military veterans were not all Marines, were not by any means few in number. They did and do, however, have every right to be proud. As do the veterans of the armed forces from time past and up through today. This book speaks most assuredly of pride. Not theirs, however, but that of those who have been served by them. We thank you. You fill our hearts with pride.

William E. Slattery

William Slattery, this editor's first cousin, served in the Navy as an aviator in the Pacific Theater during World War II and remained in the naval reserves retiring in 1966 with the rank of Lieutenant Commander. Such dry summary, however, fails to reveal the heart of Bill Slattery. Born in 1922, he entered the Navy in 1942 and earned his pilot's wings at Pensacola. Eventually stationed on the USS Chandeleur, a seaplane tender with the VPB 21 squadron, Bill flew missions over occupied China as well as along the Japanese coastline. His proudest moment came when his crew and one other were selected to drop the terms of surrender onto Wake island, officially informing the Japanese garrison there of the war's official end.

His service to his country, his state, and city did not end there. Upon returning from the Pacific in 1946, Bill enlisted in the New York City Police Department and served with the Traffic division for many years. In 1958 he took and passed the sergeant's exam and three years later was promoted to Lieutenant. Again, three years later in 1974 came his promotion to Captain. During his time with Traffic he was struck by a cab while on duty at the Canal Street Tunnel and suffered injuries which have plagued him since. One of the various ironies of wartime and peacetime service. One may survive service in the Pacific Theater of WWII without a scratch only to be seriously injured on the streets of his home town. Anyway, Bill continued on as the first commander of the Parking Enforcement Squad, eventually retiring in 1975 as Precinct Commander.

As noteworthy as the above may be, to this writer, William Slattery's most significant service has been to his family. He married Elsie Gengenbach before deployment to the Pacific and they eventually had five children: Eileen, Gene, Bill, Susan, and Chuck. Often it seems, the demands of family and career drain individuals of their sense of adventure, at least of the energy necessary to pursue uncommon ends. Such was not the case with Bill and Elsie. The year 1990 may be most remembered historically for the fall of the Berlin Wall, as symbolic of the eventual disintegration of the Soviet Union. Again Bill Slattery was on the spot. Not in Berlin. Not as a naval officer. Rather, he his beloved brother Gene, and their wives toured Russia at a time one might easily classify as perilous.

This, however, pales in comparison to a summer-long trip, the two families had undertaken earlier. From coast to coast, Great Lakes to Gulf of Mexico they traveled, camping all the way. Bill's family particularly roughed it. Mother, Father and all five children rode the miles in a station wagon barely big enough to accommodate them and their gear. Gene and his wife Barbara were more comfortable, voyaging in a car with only two children. Despite any discomfort, however, Bill and Elsie, gave their children a gift beyond reckoning. Bill's sons and daughters remember the journey with a joy such as only love and mutual respect may engender.

From this base of familial unity has grown an event by which Bill memorializes his Elsie's passing in the year 2000. On the anniversary of her birth each spring he hosts a gathering of the family which is attended in increasing numbers each year. The first of these in 2001 was small and limited to immediate children, grandchildren, local uncles and aunts who gathered for a celebratory Mass followed by lunch. As time went by, however, it grew to about one-hundred-fifty participants who gather every March at West Point. Many of us would never meet, let alone connect in any meaningful way were it not for Elsie Slattery's Mass at the Academy Catholic Chapel followed by an elaborate brunch. I personally, as do those of us living upstate, thank Bill Slattery for assembling the scattered individuals our lives prompt us to become into a family with memories and laughter, shared heritage, and love. Thank you,

Cousin. As my father once told me. "Bill Slattery is the best of us all."

Jack Madden

Jack Madden was born in 1924, graduated from LaSalle Institute in 1942, and enlisted in the U.S. Navy in 1943. His World War II service included stints aboard a P.T. Boat and later a destroyer. He returned to civilian life in 1946, but, a result of the Korean Conflict, was called to serve once more in 1950 as a Gunner's Mate second class aboard first a destroyer and later a destroyer escort.

In between wars Jack graduated with a BS. in Economics from St. Catherine of Siena college and in 1968 earned an MBA from the same school. More importantly to him, he also met and married Sophia, the love of his life and mother of his four daughters and two sons.

Both the Navy and his family loom large in the picture of who Jack Madden is. He volunteers as part of the crew maintaining the USS Slater (DE-766), a retired WWII destroyer escort launched May 1, 1944, and which as a result of the Truman Doctrine, served for a time as part of the Greek Navy. Upon her decommissioning, the Slater was adopted by the Destroyer Escort Sailors Association, refurbished, and docked at Albany,

New York where she is a popular tourist attraction. In 1998, the Slater was listed on the National Register of Historic Places. Through his association with the Slater, Jack Madden maintains close ties with former sailors, as well as helping to keep alive reminders of the times and campaigns which have made our society possible.

On the home front, Jack's Sophia has passed as has one of his sons, but they remain alive in his memory and in his heart. They are gone and he misses them. They are not, however, any further away than had they temporarily moved to some out of the way place from which someday they would return or to which Jack would eventually travel.

Since his retirement from GMAC in 1982, Jack Madden has earned a Master's Degree in Theology from St. Bernard's of Siena Institute, but that intellectual achievement does little more than signify an abiding interest in the life of the soul which in Jack is the true life, a reality so far beyond the physical that human death is no more than a necessary stage in the development from biology to spirit, from child of God to mature and accomplished son or daughter of a most proud father. Sophia lives. His son lives, as do all who have gone before.

Jack Madden is a believer of the first order. This belief, spirituality, if you will, according to Jack, first

arose while he was a child in Our Lady of Victory Parish. It has been profoundly informed by love, duty, joy, the reality of war, and the great sorrow of his later losses. He has become a unique and blessed human being. But his is not the isolated introspection of the mystic. Jack shares his awareness of higher reality through many forms of
outreach. He is a Lector in Sacred Heart Parish, carries Communion to shut-ins, is an initiate of Cursillo, and has taught in the Rite of Christian Initiation of Adults (RCIA) for several decades. Most important for him, however, was his first meeting more than forty years ago with another veteran, Army Major Pat Donohue, who was in Troy attending Rensselaer Polytechnic Institute and who introduced Jack and several others to the Christian Family Movement (CFM).

Jack states that CFM "brought Jesus to him and others," and that through CFM he was able to be part of a community of lay-people, Catholics all, who, in a break with church traditions of hundreds of years, led discussion, engaged in their personal scriptural interpretations, and who put Christ ahead of the hierarchy, the Magisterium, and truly embraced the Vatican II focus upon the individual conscience. During an interview Jack showed this writer two books from that movement: *Man and Woman,* and *The Developing Human Community.*

At the beginning of each is the simple phrase: **To Live Is Christ**. Former Gunner's Mate Jack Madden is alive.

John Henry Gray

John Henry, "Jack," Gray grew up an abandoned child in the Hillside Home in Troy, New York. His childhood was unhappy, and, by modern standards, he was abused. But, he was also made strong. An Army veteran of the Korean Conflict, Jack returned to the city of his birth, first serving as a Rensselaer County Sherriff's deputy and eventually becoming part of the Troy Police Force wherein he served for over thirty years. Now, many men and women become officers of the law, but few if any rise to a level one may call heroic. Jack did.

During his police career he was awarded 87 Commendations for Excellence in Police Duty, and was awarded the Troy Police Benevolent Association's Silver Shield Award for Bravery in 1967 and 1983. In 1967 Jack was cited for Heroism by the New York City Police Dept., the New York County Grand Jury, and the late Sen. Robert F. Kennedy. These awards were presented as the result of an incident which occurred in December 1966. While in New York City for a holiday shopping trip with his wife Colleen, Officer Gray, emerged from a subway station in the vicinity of Bryant

Park only to confront a gunman firing a rifle. The gunman had killed two people and wounded three others. After assuring Colleen's safety, Officer Gray drew his own weapon, shot and apprehended the gunman.

As the capstone of his distinguished career, In 1985 Jack Gray was inducted into the American Police Hall of Fame. These awards and deeds of valor, however, tell only part of his story, illustrate but one side of a multifaceted man of dignity, duty, and love. Jack was never a Boy Scout, but the virtues catalogued in the Scout Law apply to this extraordinary man. Jack was Trustworthy, Loyal, Helpful, Friendly, Courteous, Kind, Obedient [usually], Cheerful, Thrifty [not so much], Brave, Clean, and Reverent. If Jack had something you wanted, it was yours. If you needed a hand, he'd open both arms. And always Jack would lay his heart on the line for those he loved.

While not a gentle man, John Henry Gray was a Gentleman, a Nobleman, and a blessing to those of us who knew him.

John F.

John F., AKA "Hollywood John," is a twenty-two year veteran of the Marine Corps. He retired in1972 as a Gunnery Sergeant, who in his own words had, "traveled to damn near every country in this world and [didn't] remember one of them." His service both in Korea and Vietnam was exemplary, but his supreme achievement has come since retirement. By all accounts he is an actor, a member of SAG and Equity, but neither Korea nor Vietnam was the field of his greatest battle, nor were the studio and the stage the settings of his triumph.

This writer knows John well. He does have a last, and very Irish, name. He does not choose to reveal it. You see, his greatest trial came at the end of his enlistment and continues today. His victory will only be assured upon his death. John is an alcoholic. John has saved my life and the lives of multitudes, hundreds for certain, I would guess even thousands, with his message of hope and love, his firm hand, his Boot Camp recovery program of ninety meetings in ninety days. And then a lifetime more.

Yes, the Marines were his world for a time. The things he learned over twenty-two years of service served him well. The saying, *Once a Marine always a Marine*, stands true for John F. But he has become so much more. The Corps gave him his training. Prepared him for the conflicts to come. He would not object to my adding: God and A.A. have made him one of the very brightest of those thousand points of light President Bush once referred to.

In my eyes John F. is a hero of the highest order.

Hugh J. Blake

Hugh Blake works at Country True Value Hardware in North Greenbush, NY. His car is distinguishable in the employees' parking by its Veteran's license plate. Indeed, Hugh is most profoundly a US Army retiree having served thirty-three years and attaining the rank of Sergeant Major. Mr. Blake is a friendly man and a valuable employee. But then, so are many of us, non-veterans included. No great number of military personnel attain the rank of Sergeant Major, but then, neither do a great number of Baccalaureate degree recipients achieve a PhD.

As a soldier, Hugh excelled. His areas of service included Personnel, Aircraft Refueling, Stock Clerk, Supply, and Transportation. He also served in Iraq during 2005. His philosophy relative to deployment is simple and profound. He states flatly, "A soldier's purpose is to go to war. He trains to go to war so that his sons and grandsons don't have to." The father of a son and a daughter, grandfather of eight and great grandfather of one (so far), Hugh has done his duty in that regard, and despite recent developments, he believes that in Iraq they were, "Making a difference."

No Rambo, no Hometown Hero of any extravagant sort, Hugh and his wife of thirty-three years would seem to be leading the life of the quietly retired and the justifiably, while quietly, proud. His time has come to sit back, put up his feet, open a beer and become a devoted fan of some sports team. And, of course, to apply his considerable personal talents to being a great and great-great grandfather.

Editors do not look to such people for examples of exceptionality. Hugh, quiet, refined Hugh, would seem too average.

But can a Sergeant Major possibly be average?

The answer is No!

This writer's first hint concerning the exceptionality of Hugh Blake should have been this rank. However, it was not. One early morning before the store's opening, I happened upon Hugh in the parking lot. He was wearing a New York Marathon windbreaker. Often people wear clothing advertising the achievements or associations of others, and so, I asked. "You ran New York City?"

His reply was "Twice," a statement which he later amended. It seems during the second run he "tore [his] knee up and only did half." Further conversation revealed his finishing eight others: (1) The World Veterans' games — for runners over forty — which runs from Buffalo to Niagara Falls, Ontario, (2-3) The Niagarathon over the same course, (4-5) Buffalo, (6-7) The Country Music Marathon in Nashville, and (8) Chicago. Hugh became both a Sergeant Major and a Major Marathoner in this writer's estimation.

So, I asked more.

Hugh's time as veteran rather than active duty soldier has been anything other than retirement from the world and his duties as a citizen. As he so simply puts it. "The Army equals country. Volunteering equals community." In this latter situation Mr. Blake continues to excel as once he did in the former. He stated that once back from Iraq, while suffering "somewhat" from PTSD, his main difficulty with transition was "going from routine to free form." His initial motivation for employment three days a week at True Value was "boredom." Inactivity does not suit Hugh.

As part of his overcoming ennui, he volunteers for Melvin Rhodes Bingo which benefits the American Legion and its various projects. He also drives for Nassau Ambulance and is a Fire Police Captain for the Nassau Fire Department. In other words, as he has always done, he is giving himself to the community he is a part of. I am proud to know Hugh. He is not an average anything. That is unless one is willing to accept that so much like the others on this list, in the company of heroes and of the highly exceptional, Hugh J. Blake fits a most uncommon common mold.

A.S.

Master Sergeant A. S. chooses not to allow use of her full name for different reasons than does John F. She is an active female member of the Air Guard and for the sake of security and her personal privacy prefers to remain anonymous. She is, nonetheless, very real and very accomplished. To date she has served seventeen years in the Guard and has been deployed to Kuwait, Saudi Arabia, and, most recently to Afghanistan. These experiences have allowed her, while first and foremost serving the national interest, to gain an understanding of other cultures and, in this observer's judgment, to develop a mature and sophisticated view of several pressing issues facing humanity in the twenty-first century. Particularly in Kuwait, the issue of women's circumstances, roles, rights, and standing assumed an immediate urgency. For instance, while visiting the marketplace, the women, American military all, were looked upon with disapproval if they walked in front of the men. Kuwaiti women are expected to trail several paces behind. Also, the women were expected to remain fully covered from head to toe even in the heat. Overall, she found Kuwait a positive experience, and, while she gives no evidence of campaigning to change their culture so that it more closely resembles ours, the differences still stand clear in her mind, and, as would be most modern American women, she is thankful for the rights and freedoms women enjoy in the United States.

A.S., who enlisted while still in high school, expects to maintain a career in the Air Guard totaling twenty-five to thirty years and hopes to retire as Senior Master Sergeant. She states that the military has given her confidence, leadership skills, discipline, and a sense of pride in "who I am and what I am." And when asked what could possibly come after a life-creating experience such as this, she readily offered her hopes for a husband and family as well as a new focus, not so far removed after all from her role in the Air Guard.

Upon retirement, she hopes to have acquired the education and certification necessary to work with veterans, especially those suffering from PTSD and to focus primarily upon those who are reluctant to seek out help. Master Sergeant A.S. sees herself as especially qualified to relate to, empathize with, council, and help to heal those veterans who find few who wish to listen, and even fewer who understand. A.S. will most certainly do both. Relative to the *New York Times* article, "Despite Gains in Military, Women in War Battle to Fit In" (Carey, B., May 25, 2015), which refers to the fact that 38 percent of female service personnel suffer from post-deployment depression compared with 32 percent of men, and that the suicide rate for female soldiers triples during deployment, a woman veteran who has experienced the same stresses, doubts, and fears as have those she will counsel such A. S., will be an invaluable asset to returning veterans and through them to society as a whole.

Over the course of my tenure at Hudson Valley Community College, it has been an honor and privilege as well as great pleasure to have met many serious, dedicated, and intelligent students, not all of them veterans, but many, such as A.S., prominently so. She stated during the interview, as noted above, that the military provided her with various experiences, instilled within her qualities such as discipline and confidence, and functioned significantly in the creation of the person she is today. As I reflect upon students past and present, A.S. stands out as a person of great quality who will achieve her stated goals, and, should such be the full extent of her human development, she will have been a positive force and have exerted lasting influence upon the world and the people around her. I do believe, however, that in her time, as all our times pass and change in ways we cannot anticipate, A.S. is destined to do more than she yet realizes. As Shakespeare said in

Twelfth Night, "Be not afraid of greatness. Some are born great, some achieve greatness, and others have greatness thrust upon them." I expect great things from Master Sergeant A.S. She shows all the signs.

Reference:

Carey, Benedict (2015, May 25, 2015). Despite Gains, Women in War Battle to Fit In. *The New York Times*, pp.A1, A10.

James J Slattery

June 2016

1.
I LOOK FORWARD TO MEETING HIM

To Whom It May Concern: Saverio John Rea, on June 9, 1943, died as a result of a crash when his plane was shot down near Espiritu Santo, New Hebrides. He entered into the Marine Corps on March 11, 1942. A telegram, with this information, arrived at his family's house while his mother was at a funeral. He was nineteen years old.

This happened before I was born. I never met "Sonny" and didn't know him yet I feel emotional pain when thinking about him. When I reflect longer I realize that he has been with me all of my life and I know him very well. I know him because his name has been a part of the acronym on the veterans club located about two blocks from our childhood home on Hill Street. It is now called the CARB club. When I was a kid it was called the CRAB club. My parents, relatives and friends went there for many social gatherings. His image is at the club with the other men from Troy, New York who were some of the first to lose their lives in World War II – Cicarelli, Agars, Rea and Bevevino.

I know him because I have seen his picture many times. One with a young lady while home on leave at a wedding. He looked so handsome in uniform, like a movie star. I have also seen a picture of his marine graduating class and the one that you see in this column. I know him because of the stories told by his sisters, Josephine and Kay. They smile when they say those nice things that we usually say about anyone who is deceased but, in this case, you can tell that it is not made up. Most often they mention how loving he was to his mother, Josephine. They also mentioned that at the time of his death the "the family completely fell apart."

I know him because I hear the stories of veterans twice a month as I co-facilitate support groups for veterans and their families at the First Unitarian Universalist Church in Albany. The veterans are from all wars since World War II. Obviously, they are different from Saverio but the stories seem remarkably similar – replete with pain, anguish and horror.

I know him really well because I have letters that he sent to his younger sister and cousin while in the service. One of them has a postmark that says, Paris Island 1942. Below are some of his randomly selected words that at times are filled with advice, compassion, longing and regret. "Dear Sis, I really don't know how to start." "Josephine, stop and think of what a great mother we have. The way she thinks of others and goes out of her way to help them." "Dad and I had our misunderstandings. I want you to know why." "The first thing I am going to do when I get home is to apologize to dad and ask for forgiveness as only a descent son would." "Writing helps me to unload a lot of my feelings." "Don't be afraid to ask mom and dad for advice. Go to them whenever you are troubled." "Take care of Katy (younger sister). She loves you like I love both of you." The letters gave me the feeling that he knew his fate.

I know him because we share the parts of the same name. My name is John Rea Ostwald. He was my mother's brother and my uncle. I look forward to meeting him in the afterlife.

2.
PATRIOT FLIGHT: TRIP OF HONOR FOR THE GREATEST GENERATION

A few weeks ago on an ugly, rainy morning at 5:45 am, mom and I drove to the Sam's Club parking lot in Latham, New York. I wondered why we were meeting there because we were flying out of the Albany airport in about an hour or so. My question was answered when I saw the half-mile entourage of Law Enforcement Personnel, Firefighters, Patriot Guard Riders and numerous other well-wishers. I have heard about this great, altruistic endeavor before, The Patriot Flight; now we were a part of it. Ironically, the man who started it all, William Peak, was the Grand Marshal of the Flag Day parade last week.

This was a great beginning to a magnificent adventure and one of the many times that we would feel like celebrities on this trip. Our bus, filled with veterans and family members, pulled into the airport shortly after 6:30 and there was an eruption of cheering, flashing lights, and applause. Subsequently, we were escorted into the baggage area for an opening ceremony. It was a wonderful and touching event. Linda Weiss, the Director of the VA Hospital, was one of the speakers. She spoke passionately about her dad and veterans in general. After the other, brief but meaningful speeches, the vets were introduced individually. Out of the thirty plus veterans, my mom was the only female WW II veteran there that day so she got an extra loud applause.

Other Highlights of the trip:

When we arrived at the Baltimore airport, the crowd at the gate yelled and cheered with excitement. We were startled but humbled by the response of the group of over two hundred strangers who took time out to honor their heroes.

After a short bus ride, we arrived at an area where most of the war monuments were. There was another brief ceremony, more picture taking and recalling of the events of over a half century ago. I saw my buddy Mike O'Connor's name on the Viet Nam memorial just like it is on the wall in downtown Troy.

Mom left pictures of her and her brother at the base of a monument that were to be picked up and sent to the Smithsonian Institute. These words were written on the back, "My dear brother, you are always in my thoughts more and more as time goes by. I will see you and be with you someday. Love your sister, Josephine."

A few days before the trip I told a friend that I was going and she said that she had been on the flight with her dad. Here are some comments about her adventure.

"It was a stellar experience escorting my father Bill a WWII Army Ranger of the 6th Ranger Battalion in the Philippines, and his high school best friend Mike, a WWII Navy mechanic, on the flight. The impromptu heartfelt gratitude and public reactions to these true heroes was incredible to witness. I was so privileged to experience their reactions, surprise, and happiness in participating in the flight to the WWII monument."

The leaders on the trip coordinate the flights, do the fund-raising, and keep everything in order. It was obvious to anyone there that these people had a genuine caring and affection for vets. One summed up the experience very well when he said, "It is a trip of honor for the greatest generation."

John Ostwald

3.
HELPING HIM TELL HIS STORY

Ann Marie asked me to interview her father, on video tape, so her family could have a permanent record of his recollections of WW II. She first approached me with this idea at a family picnic on the Fourth of July. I looked forward to speaking with her father, Dominic, to plan our meeting in the near future.

Dominic and Edith live at a Senior Housing facility. As I walked into their apartment and was greeted with warm hugs. Our families have known each other for decades. They used to live on Fourth Street, across the street from my grandfather, Pat Zucaro's liquor store. I learned later that Dom was originally from 5th Avenue where he grew up with five brothers and two sisters. He is a real Troy boy.

Ann Marie had set up a camera to record the interview and left a note on how to operate the device. She also mentioned some topics that her dad may leave out. I goofed around with the camera controls, moved some chairs and felt confident that it was going to go okay. Dom and I were in two chairs next to each other. We were ready to go. After I pressed the red record button, I said the date, who I was and the primary purpose of the interview. Next I had Army Corporal Dominic Farina ,of the 576th Ordnance Ammunition Company stationed in Ardens,

Germany, show his medals and two 8x10 pictures of himself; one current and the other as a young army private. We talked about a variety of topics including how he got into the war, leaving home, getting orders for Europe, seeing the result of atrocities, witnessing bombing runs, and the often boring day-to-day patrols. Ann Marie told me to have him mention a cook that he was friends with. Dom laughed hardily when he talked about a southerner who called him "you little guinea." Dom is 5'5" and many of you are familiar with this slang term for an Italian. Dom got on his friend's good side and was given all the potatoes and eggs he wanted.

Dom also recalled the issues related to the Battle of the Bulge and being an extra in an Army Training movie with some other GIs. Through most of the interview, he laughed and his eyes danced as he recounted his experiences but there were interruptions in his mood when he again mentioned the traumatic experiences of war – wounded paratroopers, hundreds of dead Jewish civilians, and bombs exploding. Near the end of the interview, I got his wife Edith on camera for a few minutes. She was very camera shy when compared to her extroverted, jocular husband.

A few days later at about 9:30 am, I got a call from cousin Vicenza. She said that Ann Marie had asked her to call me and report that Dominic had died. She said he just sat in the back seat of the car and that was it; he was gone. I was stunned, surprised and glad all at the same time. I just saw Dom's smiling face and vibrant presentation three days ago. Now he was in the afterlife. I recall his laugh and I thought that I heard him say. "Lucky we did this in time."

I viewed the interview on disc a few times to enable me to complete this column. My head was cut off from the screen but it didn't matter. I was lucky enough to be able to help an honorable man tell his story.

4.
CARING MEANS SHARING THE BURDEN

When I pulled onto a small road near Craryville, New York and saw the sign, Pumpkin Hollow, I knew that my journey to Viet Nam was really beginning. About three months ago, I was invited by Dr. Ed Tick to join him and others on his eighth trip to Viet Nam. The primary purpose of these trips is to promote healing for Viet Nam vets and their families. The gathering at Pumpkin Hollow was a four-day seminar, organized by Soldier's Heart, an organization founded by Dr. Tick and Kate Dahlsted. It was primarily for service providers and therapists who wanted to learn more about Post Traumatic Stress Disorder and other concerns that develop when human beings experience the inhumanity of war.

Pumpkin Hollow is a serene, spiritual sanctuary that hosts a variety of meetings. The small stone walls that border the meditation garden, the fast moving stream and simple but immaculate rooms make it seem like an odd place to talk about the horrors of war. I could only stay for dinner and the opening ceremony but it was just enough time to meet some of my fellow travelers. There are about 18 of us leaving for the Far East in October. The group includes vets, supportive family members, therapists and a film crew who are working on an Agent Orange documentary.

During dinner, I met some people who have traveled great distances to learn how to help, not only Viet Nam vets, but those of another generation who will be returning from Iraq and Afghanistan. Kaye, Bill and Stacey came from Atlanta, Lisa from Chicago and Lance from Tucson to name a few.

After dinner, we met in the octagon shaped meditation center. Ed and Kate greeted us warmly and reviewed plans for the next few days. After the introduction and an "icebreaker" exercise, Ed spoke about how current societies don't know how to support their returning warriors. A short time later Ed asked all the vets to stand up. The group of about forty people chanted, sang, applauded and beat drums to honor us. Dr. Ed Tick has been working with victims of trauma for over twenty-five years. He has developed treatments that are unique and also expands on traditional approaches. In addition to "honoring the warriors," he strongly advocates bringing the demons up from the depths of the heart and soul so they can be confronted. Ed's theories and treatment approaches are detailed in his book, "War and the Soul."

After the opening ceremony, I met my roommate for the Viet Nam journey. His name is Stephen. He explained that he was not a veteran but was going to Viet Nam to try and find the place where his brother died. He showed me a picture of the handsome 22 year old that was taken just before he left home. A few weeks after I met Stephen I was on a planned trip to Washington D.C. When I approached the Viet Nam memorial, I called Stephen, got his brother's name and took a picture where the name was inscribed on the wall. At this moment, I got an eerie feeling that led me to believe that, sometime soon, Stephen and I were going to be standing at the approximate spot, in Viet Nam, were his brother died.

This is the first in a series of columns that I will submit intermittently over the next few months until we leave in October. During the following weeks, I will be reading, packing, planning and doing some fund-raising for the trip. To use an overused phrase, for me this is the "opportunity of a life time." I will be able to support combat vets who now have the courage to face the formidable demons that have plagued them for decades. I will also learn more about myself and the forgiving nature of the Vietnamese people

Dr. Ed Tick concluded the opening ceremony of the seminar by saying, "Caring means sharing the burden." Yes, we all have a responsibility to share in the healing of our warriors.

Vietnam Healing
Trip 2008

5.
EXCITEMENT, APPREHENSION AHEAD

I have my passport, visa, and insect repellant. Maureen and Carole, at the County Health department, made sure that I got the Hepatitis A, B and typhoid shots. Today, I'm going to fill the prescription for the malaria pills that I have to start taking the week before we leave for Viet Nam. Donna at Dr. Benjamin's office gave me a bunch of dental supplies for the kids in Viet Nam just like she did a few years ago when I went to Africa. One of the two suitcases that I bring will be completely filled with donations. I borrowed my son's digital camera and bought a few disposables cameras just in case anything goes wrong with the technological wonder or its operator.

I have read a lot of books and seen both documentary and commercial films on the Viet Nam war. Watching the documentaries was starting to give me nightmares so I stopped. I just finished a four-day intensive training led by Dr. Edward Tick and Kate Dahlsted, from Soldier's Heart located in Troy. My entire sabbatical has been spent learning more about

Post Traumatic Stress Disorder. This is a serious problem that affects many service men and women coming back from Iraq and Afghanistan in addition to the Viet Nam vets that will be on the journey with us.

We leave on Oct. 14 at about 2 pm from the Albany airport. I thought that you might find our itinerary interesting. It includes many unique experiences. When we go to the Mekong Delta, our hosts will be Viet Cong veterans, a husband and wife. We will visit shrines, victims of Agent Orange and a beautiful countryside. Departure US Oct 14, arrive Oct 163 days and nights in Ho Chi Minh City (Saigon). 2 days, 1 night in Mekong Delta. 2 days, 1 night in Tay Ninh province (Cu Chi, Black Lady Mtn., Cao Dai, etc.), overnight in Saigon again. 2 days in Pleiku - one night in Montegnaard village, one in Pleiku town, 3 days and nights in Hoi An, with visits to Tam Ky, My Lai, Da Nang and a day off to rest. 1 day and night in Dong Ha and old DMZ area, 3 days and nights in Ha Noi last days and overnight on a boat in the exquisite Ha Long Bay with visit to Rosy Jade Humanity Center, rehab for Agent Orange disabled fly home Nov. 1.

As the time nears, I am excited and apprehensive about this new adventure. Excited because of travel to a new land filled with mysterious and awesome beauty. Excited because of the new things that I will learn about a foreign culture. Apprehensive because of anticipating the depth of pain that some vets will experience.

6.
HEALING THE WOUNDS OF WAR

Paul and Denise left from Albany International Airport on October 19th at 4 am. They are going to Vietnam. It has been 35 years since Paul has been in Vietnam. Denise, his wife, has never been there.

I interviewed Paul in his office before he left. His office is filled with memorabilia from past wars – pictures, medals, helmets and even uniforms. Paul has helped countless vets navigate the confusing and sometimes inadequate. He has also spent countless hours providing emotional support to vets traumatized by their unique, tragic experiences. Now it was Paul's turn to confront the demons that have tortured him since 1972.

I asked Paul how this trip came about. He said that it evolved through conversations with Dr. Ed Tick, the noted Psychotherapist/Author, who has brought many soldiers and their loved ones to Vietnam for healing. Ed has been working with Vets for over 30 years. His website, www.soldiersheart.net, states, "The mission of Soldier's Heart is to heal the wounds of war, educate our communities about the trauma of war, and help veterans re-integrate with their families and communities."

Ed Tick's book, War and the Soul (2005) also presents ways, "to nurture a positive warrior identity based in compassion and forgiveness." I met Ed when he gave a workshop at a college upstate. He is the only person who ever said to me directly, "thank you for serving our country." His statement was simple yet very meaningful to me.

As my interview with Paul continued, I asked specifically why he was going. "I am tired of be haunted by images from the past." "Denise has been pushing me for years to do something more about my Post Traumatic Stress Disorder." "I need to do this." As a young Marine, Paul exhibited courage when facing the enemy in battle. Now, years later, a new kind of courage was necessary. The courage that transcends war experiences – the courage to face oneself. When questioned about his expectations, Bob said, "Most people tell me that it is not like it was before." "The Vietnamese are friendly and it has been a positive experience for veterans who return there."

Paul also related that he had been feeling "a great deal of anxiety" but now, three days before his departure, the nervousness has turned to excitement. His feelings of dread may have decreased because of conversations with other guys going on the trip. He will hook up with most of them in California. This is Paul's new "Band of Brothers".

The depth of the relationship between comrades who have served in the armed forces is difficult to comprehend. Paul gave us a significant insight into this bond when he said, "We will be going to Saigon, Da Nang, Hanoi, Marble Mountain, China Beach and I will be going to My Lai for Mark." Paul was referring to his friend, Mark, a well known bar owner who died in 2000. Mark was an Army vet who also suffered from the emotional wounds of an unpopular war.
I spoke to Denise a few days later. She said that she was

going with her husband, "to learn more about the important experiences in Paul's life." Denise said that she was excited about learning about other cultures and at the same time concerned for Paul. She concluded by saying that she is optimistic, confident and centered. In the book, Vietnam: and American Ordeal, the author, George Donelson Moss, states "Vietnam veterans returning home in the sixties and seventies rarely received parades or official welcomes home. Few Americans appeared to appreciate their sacrifice or thanked them for a job well done. They were often ignored by a society that had carelessly sent them off to fight a war that most Americans were ambivalent about or had lost faith in completely."

We hope that when Paul returns on November 7th his welcome home will be different than the one he didn't receive over three decades ago.

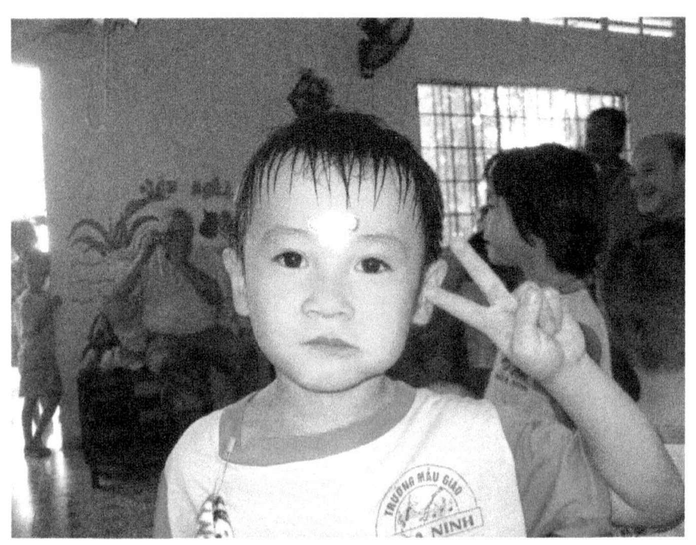

7.
DISCOVERING PEACE AND HEALING

We are leaving for Viet Nam on Tuesday. I have explained to my mom why we are going and that it won't be dangerous, but she still has questions. I figured the best way to educate her is to ask Dr. Ed Tick to write her a letter answering her questions more completely. Ed is the director of Soldier's Heart based in Troy. This will be his eighth journey to Viet Nam. Here is his answer to my mother.

"Dear Josephine, The Viet Nam War (which the Vietnamese call The American War) ended in 1975. Yet it is remarkable how war imprints frightening images in our minds. This can be true for civilians as well as veterans. On one trip, the daughter of a combat veteran traveled with me to make peace with her father's story. The father implored me to "not let my daughter jump out of any choppers into hot landing zones."

Even three decades and more after service, some veterans can only imagine Viet Nam still at war. Some ache to return and make peace. Others claim they could never go back because they "could not stand the smell of war again."

"Many civilians blanch or their eyes tear up when I tell them I am going to Viet Nam. They still feel deep grief and confusion over that war. One college student recently said, "I didn't know Viet Nam was a country. I thought it was just the name of a war." Veterans and civilians alike remain woefully unaware of the country and people against whom we waged a twelve-year war.

Viet Nam is a country with a rich, diverse, beautiful and ancient heritage. Its capital, Hanoi, will celebrate its 1000th anniversary in 2010. Viet Nam has a deep, abiding spiritual heritage that comes from several sources -- Buddhism, Taoism, Confucianism, and ancestor worship.

This creates a people with a remarkable capacity to accept struggles without blame, forgive, reconcile, live in the present, honor all people, and not hold grudges. They are also primarily an agrarian people, dependent on the land and still living in traditional ways.

In Viet Nam we will meet people, including Viet Cong and North Vietnamese Army veterans, who welcome, love, forgive and accept us. One elderly woman, the only one in her family to survive the infamous My Lai massacre, said, "I believe that the only reason I survived was so I could take American veterans' hands, look into their eyes, forgive them and help them heal."

"Why should your son go to Viet Nam? Will he be safe? All Americans need to learn that there is no more war in Viet Nam, that forgiveness and reconciliation are possible, and that we can live in friendship and cooperation all over the planet. Combat veterans often experience full healing of their war disorders from such encounters. Ironically, today Viet Nam is one of the SAFEST places on the planet for Americans to visit.

During the Vietnam War era, your son served our country with honor but he never had to serve in Viet Nam. On this journey, he will be safe, welcomed, and honored by the Vietnamese. Along with the rest of our visiting Americans, he will serve his time in country by helping his brother veterans and others discover peace and bring healing to both countries.

The war is long over and the Vietnamese have healed their country and moved on. What better way to learn that than to visit? What a better way to transform the images of war that we Americans carry in our minds than to see for yourself a country and people who love and practice peace?"

After mom read the letter, she was both relieved and happy. I look forward to telling her all about the trip when I return.

8.
TRIP TO VIET NAM DEEPLY MOVING

We left Ha Long Bay after a day of rest and recuperation to start the trip back to the USA. After 30 hours of bus and plane travel and lay overs, we were home. Yes, it is definitely a hike from Viet Nam to Taipei, China to San Francisco to JFK to Albany. Imagine what it was like for the thousands of vets who travelled this route decades ago to fight unfamiliar people in an unfamiliar land in an unpopular war.

Our itinerary for this trip was ambitious. Dr. Edward Tick and Kate Dahlsted, co-directors of Soldier's Heart, wanted to give vets and family members the opportunity to honor their dead and continue the grieving process. In addition, a film crew, working on the Agent Orange film, "A Permanent Mark", had scheduled a series of important interviews and activities.

We started in the South at Saigon (Ho Chi Minh City), and made our way north to Hanoi. We went to places that I've read about or watched on the Discovery Channel but never thought that I would actually see like the Mekong Delta, Tah Ninh Province, Pleiku, Hoi An, Dong Ha, My Lai, Hue, Da Nang, and the central highlands. It was emotionally and physically challenging. Old wounds were opened once more but spirits were also renewed.

A wife honored her husband who brought death home from Viet Nam in the form of an Agent Orange related cancer. A man from Seattle honored the site were his older brother died with prayers, Native American chanting and incense burning. An American vet, still plagued with survivor guilt, honored his "brother" who was killed by friendly fire as they huddled close to one another in a foxhole. These people, and others on the trip, displayed the courage to explore the shattered glass and smoldering ashes of their damaged hearts. It was real courage.

I was deeply moved by some of the experiences, especially a trip to the My Lai museum at the site where 504 unarmed farm families were killed by American Forces. Proof once again that war produces unique tragedies more often than opportunities for heroism.

Another unique tragedy was the devastation caused by Agent Orange. It has affected not only the frail North Vietnamese vets, but many young children. Like most people in the US, when I think of Agent Orange I usually think of aging vets, not kids. It is assumed that the contamination from this herbicide will effect at least five generations of the Vietnamese people.

After seeing some of the extreme damage caused by the war and after reading the critically acclaimed books "The Sorrow of War" and "Last Night I Dreamed of Peace" I found myself tearfully apologizing to a group of Vietnamese for the devastation that was caused in their country.

During our second week "in country", we met with several Viet Cong veterans who had defended their land again from foreign invaders (previously the French and Chinese). The Viet Nam War was a long time ago and this was a new day for all. Animosity was absent as we saluted each other, hugged and drank rice wine. These are very forgiving people with open minds and hearts. Compassion is their way.

I returned to the USA exhausted but happy that I had the opportunity to learn more about myself and hopefully support the healing journey of others.

Welcome Home
Vietnam
Vets!!!
WELCOME HOME

9.
WELCOME AND THANKS

We were waving, cheering and displaying our banners that said "Welcome Home Vietnam Vets." As they took the turn around the security area of the airport, they saw us. The gladness and surprise on their faces illuminated the area like a bright sunshine. It was not the late sixties or early seventies. It was a Wednesday night in the new millennium. Families and supporters were there to honor those who sacrificed so valiantly decades ago. Caught up in the moment, I hugged a guy I didn't know; Leo from Albany, New York. Soon after, I got a big hug from my friend, Paul who was also on this cathartic emotional journey. These men and others like them are warriors from the past who sought peace in a land thousands of miles from home. Their journey started with Dr. Ed Tick and Kate Dahlsted from Soldier's Heart, who have taken vets and family members to Vietnam for healing. This is their seventh trip. This is a war story but not like the ones that you are used to. It is a war story filled with compassion, forgiveness and love. The love can easily be seen between Leo and Paul who faced this challenge with unity and emotional courage. Periodically, during the trip, they faced challenges alone. They mentioned that when they encountered terrain where death had occurred, that they needed solitude to confront the ghosts and demons of their past. Paul mentioned that these experiences, although painful, created a metamorphosis. He said, "I feel reborn." Leo spoke softly but eloquently about "memorializing comrades who didn't make it." Like Paul, he said that a significant change had occurred. "I came home complete and right."

The compassion and forgiveness in this story seem to come more frequently from the Vietnamese people who blame governments more than soldiers for war. Their religion, Buddhism, supports spiritual healing while often minimizing the importance of aggressive acts against them. Paul said that he was welcomed in a village where 112 people were killed by American bombs. Vets who return to Viet Nam soon embrace this forgiving philosophy that is foreign to many Americans.

During the Veterans Day weekend there are several events honoring Vets. They are often attended by civil servants and politicians as well as the families of veterans. Our County Executive really impressed us by coming out to the airport at 11 o'clock at night after a recent, busy Election Day. This was a powerful communication. It wasn't a political thing. It was the right thing.

The day after our airport welcome, cousin Jimmy and I attended a free luncheon provided for vets by Questar III, a career technical education center. The culinary students and other young people provided a great meal and superior service. The principal and his staff should be commended for spear heading this effort now in its fourth year.

Finally, on the tables at the Questar facility were little cards with a heart surrounding an American flag. On the tiny cards was a message that really says it clearly to the Veterans and their families – "We Thank You All!"

10.
BROTHER KEN IS A HERO OF LIFE

I have written columns about women before – Stella the tailor, my cousin Vincenza, my friend Sharon from Florida, and Margarita from Brooklyn, by way of Columbia. I don't write about guys because I think that we are boring. I am breaking this pattern because I have found a worthy subject. The man I am writing about is an orphan, Viet Nam combat veteran, chaplain at a local jail and a Franciscan Brother.

Brother Ken Lucas' life began in Watertown NY at St Mary's Hospital but he mentioned that his hometown was Philadelphia, New York. When he was 18 months old, the welfare department took him, his brother, and sister away. They said that they were not getting the right care at home. Brother Ken said, "We all cried our eyes out and were hurt very much. I don't know if I really ever got over that." He spent twelve years in an orphanage and mentioned that the experiences there were, "Too painful to repeat." When he turned 18, he joined the Marine Corps. After boot camp and two and half years at Camp Pendleton, California he went to Japan for a month of raider school. His next stop was Vietnam where he saw, "The best and the worse of humanity.

"When I came home from the war there was no band or people saying welcome home – nothing. Just me standing at the airport waiting for my step dad and my mom to take me home. The people in the airport did not even know I was there. It was like I was invisible. I went home with the feeling that I just didn't matter or my best friend, who died over there, didn't matter either. He died for me and I will not forget that." Brother Ken told me that one time, when he arrived home on leave, he changed into civilian clothes in the bathroom on the bus, because he was embarrassed to be in uniform.

After his discharge from the service, Brother Ken worked for about 12 years in a factory. He said that a man at work kept saying to him, "Have you ever thought about being a brother or a priest?" "I told Him to leave me alone because I had not gone to church in a long time; not even when fighting in Vietnam. He would not leave me alone so one day after work I stopped at a church and took a seat in a pew. I saw the red light go on over the confessional and went in." I said, "Father it has been so many years; I don't know where to begin." He said, "Welcome home!" "After that experience I started to go to church regularly and three years later joined the Franciscans. Not too long after that, I began doing jail work. I have been doing it for 25 years now and when I walk into the jail, I see myself behind these bars. The rejection and anger that confused me as a child have been transformed so I can help others."

I met Brother Ken a few years ago. We have worked together, as volunteers, to help veterans adjust to civilian life. Despite all of the challenges that he has faced, he has maintains a positive attitude, great sense of humor and unlimited generosity. He is not only a hero of war; he is a hero of life.

11.
THOUGHTS OF 911 AND IRAQ

One of my students has Post Traumatic Stress Disorder. She is twenty-six years old. This is her story. "I graduated high school in 1998. At the time, I had no idea what I wanted to do with my life. My friends convinced me to talk to a recruiter and I joined the Army National Guard.

At first, I enjoyed training, and then 9/ 11 happened. We were called down to New York City to help in any way that we could. I have no words to describe the things that I saw, heard, or the smells that on occasion still linger. I was thankful that I could go home to my family, but sorry that others could not. I think that this is when the feelings of guilt and anger truly began.

In February of 2003, I was told that we were being deployed to Iraq. We arrived there in April of 2003. Every day we would run missions to Baghdad to secure the base that we established and to ensure the safety of other convoys going through the area. I cannot remember a day that I did not lock and load my weapons. We ended up losing two men while in Iraq, this is when the guilt really started and I had intense anger and hate. I wanted revenge; we all did. It got to the point that people started volunteering for night missions, where we would try to draw out the Iraqis just to have the chance to kill them. All of the missions we went on were very exciting. We never knew what would happen. Every time that I would leave the base camp, I would look around, just in case I did not see it again. I do not have too many memories that I am able to bring up anymore.

I found out in September that my husband had spent all of the money that I had earned, on his girl-friend and ruined my credit. It was tough to handle what was going on in Iraq and at home. I chose to withdraw and spend a lot of time alone. In October, I was forced to seek help by one of the officers. I was put on an anti-depressant and sleeping pills.

We eventually came home in April of 2004. At first, I would have a drink here and there, then it became seven nights a week. I liked not having to think or experience the pain or memories. I started seeing a counselor in September, and continued to see her weekly for about a year. I was told that I had Post Traumatic Stress Disorder. It was nice to finally put a name to everything I had been feeling. When I came home, I had trouble sleeping and would have night-mares about things I had seen. I had flashbacks quite often; I was always anxious and always aware of what was going on around me. I would not go to large places where I could not see everyone. I did not trust people. Any noises would put me on edge. With counseling, some of these things occur less often, but I am told that I will battle PTSD for the rest of my life. I have taken myself off of the medications because I do not want to have to depend on them to handle the stressors of life.

I still feel intense guilt because I am still alive and two wonderful men lost their lives. That is something that I deal with on a regular basis, but at least now I know that I am alive for a reason and I am able to handle the guilt. My life has gotten better since counseling. My divorce was finalized in December 2004 finally, I was free. I am doing well in school, have a job that I love, a family that I adore, and I am with someone that takes care of me and understands."

12.
A LETTER FROM IRAQ

One of my former students sent me a letter from his base in Iraq. This is his response to President Bush's State of the Union Address. It is not intended to be an antiwar piece or political statement per se but an opportunity for us to get a closer look into the heart and mind of one of our loved ones. Some of the words have been omitted for security reasons.

"I am still hoping that I will get to come home. I hate to say it but I hope that the left wing guys get what they want. I don't care about the big picture right. We have lost this war. Sending more troops would do nothing to save it. The Iraqi's don't want us here and we will never stop the insurgents. Sending more troops would only add to the death toll. I hope we pull out. This is a lost cause. There is no reason to be here. They only reason we came here is for the oil and we are not even using it"

"Bush has done a good job but he had no chance from the start. If we do pull out there will be peace. The Shiites will come to power and the Sunni's and Kurds will be slaughtered. Oh well, it is not our troops. I hope I am not shocking you too much but that is how I feel. We are not fighting a war we are driving up and down the road getting shot at and blown up. When this happens, we do nothing about it. We have two black eyes and still taking punches without defending ourselves. This deployment has shown me a lot. The reason October was the fourth bloodiest month is because of all the death from IED's, rockets and small arms fire. Our boys who we fought like hell to save civilians got slaughtered. We did our best and gave every effort we had but they still died like sheep.

I am tired. I worked myself to the ground for six months with no break and now it is time for me to come home. I don't care if the Dems or Reps are in power; I just want to be back home. I sound very desperate because I am. I am at the end of my rope. I can't do this for another one, two or even six months. We all feel the same way. I try to keep my head up but my government will not let me. They tell me I am going home then at the last minute tell me I might have to stay. If I have to stay then I will work until I feel I am not fit to. I am no good out there when I am not mentally in the game. You know I am never one to quit but there is a point where I go from fit to dangerous. That line is life or death. It would be in best interest for all when the time comes. I couldn't go through another deployment. I would lose my mind if I had to bury one of the guys I am with now. That would be the straw that broke my back. Well I hope you are not mad but this is how I feel. "I spoke to this vet's mom after I received the letter and she said," I continue to pray that he makes good decisions along the way. Deployment is a family experience, it takes patience, encouragement and many nights of worry and sometimes it just takes its toll on the ones who love them. I sent a young energetic boy over to this war and in a short period, it created a man. I hope that a man who in many years to come will be able to look back on this experience with faded memories but never to forget. This will always be a part of who he will become. God Bless them all."

13.
THE SENTENCING OF A MARINE

Last summer I brought some of my students to the sentencing of a young Marine in Federal Court on Broadway in Albany. The issues and charges were relevant to the course that I was teaching at the time - Abnormal Psychology.

After we got past the guards and metal detectors, we took some seats before the primary participants entered. Without the Judge, attorneys and other court personnel present, there was a relaxed feeling in the large room filled with priceless antique wood and supporters of the defendant. When we heard "all rise", everything changed.

After listening to passionate words from the Defense Attorney and stern parental/legal terms from the Prosecuting Attorney; the defendant spoke. Mike rose from his chair and stood at attention the same way that he was taught in the Marines. He acknowledged his wrongdoing and apologized. I tried to focus on what I was feeling about what he said versus just his words. His sincerity and regret were apparent, at least to me. A minute later I remember thinking," It doesn't matter what Mike or the attorneys say. This is a done deal." The apology, PTSD references and nothing else mattered. The judge had already decided on a sentence of 33 months. The Prosecutor mentioned treatment for Post-Traumatic Stress Disorder in prison. I worked in the Correctional System for a few years. Prisons are designed for punishment and usually enable inmates to learn more skills for crime. Adequate treatment is minimal and often nonexistent.

Mike waved to his family as the deputies escorted him out of the courtroom. Many of us were left with the obvious question, "How much of his criminal behavior was due to choice and how much to the debilitating effects of war?"

On Monday March 16 at 9 am, another Marine faces trial in state court. Kevin Murphy's conviction was reversed by the Appellate Division of the Supreme Court, Third Judicial Department. He has been in prison since April 30, 2006 after the first conviction for murder. There have been several published accounts of the death of one the alleged assailants and the subsequent trial.

(http://josepherome.personalizedmemorial.com/client/index.php?user_a=legacy

http://community.fox23news.com/forums/thread/2972956.aspx

http://community.fox23news.com/forums/permalink/3013966/2997367/ShowThread.aspx

http://www.wten.com/global/story.asp?s=5803889&ClientType=Printable

http://www.empirestatenews.net/News/20061018-7.html).

Pertinent issues in this case will probably be those reviewed in the news stories mentioned above i.e. the criminal records of the three alleged assailants, location of the crime (in front of the defendant's residence), motivation of the defendant, etc. I hope that someone will again introduce the possible effects of combat training and deployment in Iraq and Kuwait on Kevin

Murphy's psyche. Often the courts fail to understand that even if vets don't have a diagnosis of Post-Traumatic Stress Disorder, they are forever changed.

Some courts are starting to recognize the unique needs of veterans. The first veterans' court opened last year in Buffalo, N.Y.; its success stories have led to more across the country. Nicholas Riccardi reports from Tulsa, Oklahoma that U.S. military veterans from three decades pass through Judge Sarah Smith's courtroom here, reporting on their battles with drug addiction, alcoholism and despair. Her court is part of a new approach in the criminal justice system: specialized courts for veterans who have broken the law. Judges have been spurred by a wave of troops returning from Iraq and Afghanistan, battling post-traumatic stress disorder and brain injuries and stumbling into trouble with the law. But advocates of the courts say they also address a problem as old as combat itself.

"Some families give their sons or daughters to service for their country, and they're perfectly good kids. And they come back from war and just disintegrate before our eyes," said Robert Alvarez, a counselor at Ft. Carson in Colorado who is advocating for a veterans court in the surrounding county. "Is it fair to put these kids in prison because they served and got injured?"

Finally, when our government doesn't give enough serious and careful thought before sending our young people to war it is our responsibility to change judicial processes to meet the unique and important needs of returning vets.

U.S. ARMY
ARMY

14.
STUDENT VETERANS NEED OUR SUPPORT

Many students will face significant challenges when school starts shortly. My twelve year old, and his peers, enter the brave new world of middle school. Students from other countries have to hone up on their English language skills and also have to adjust too many cultural differences. Older students may not have been in school for a few decades and doubt their ability to succeed. During my first week in the classroom, I sense that some students are bewildered and wondering, "What am I doing here?"

It is been my experience, as an teacher and a faculty advisor to the Armed Forces Club, that few students face as many challenges as veteran students. Their adjustment to being home and being in the college environment can be influenced by a variety of factors including:

Being and Feeling different from civilian peers. This change of identity starts in boot camp.

Abuse of Alcohol and other drugs. Some of my student veterans report that as many as eight out of ten of their friends are involved with this problem.

PTSD Symptomatology. This is a biopsychosocial issue that has been recognized since at least the Civil War. Symptoms are varied and often interfere with learning and "normal" functioning.

Depression and Suicidal Ideation/Attempts. The unprecedented suicide rate for vets and active duty personnel has received much attention in the national media.

Traumatic Brain Injuries (TBI). This physical malady, often caused by explosions, may have a variety of troubling symptoms including insomnia, memory loss and emotional instability.

Intermittent deaths of former comrades. Some of my students have found out this disturbing information on Facebook.

Frequent and unpredictable deployments. Some National Guard members and Reservists are particularly vulnerable to this interference with educational planning.

One of my colleagues, J. Daniel Beaudry, sent this comment to me recently. It gives a more personal perspective. "I think one of the profounder realizations I have had occurred when I was accompanying a student veteran to a screening of a movie documenting one military unit's deployment in Afghanistan. At one point I said to him, "As a veteran, you must now feel sort of like a hand or a leg without a body," and he responded, "Exactly." "During their training and subsequent service, members of the armed forces become a part of a larger organism, one that is capable of functioning together in such a way as to achieve goals that no single person could aspire to alone.

When veterans return to the civilian world, to a culture built on individualism, freedom of choice, and competition, they often feel alone, confused, frustrated, and, ultimately, "less than" what they once were--no longer capable of the levels of achievement once possible through comradely (community) effort." This comment really addresses the issue of feeling that one doesn't fit in many civilian environments; including the college campus."

These are some of the unique challenges faced by veterans on our campus. One might ask. How might these dilemmas affect learning, concentration and emotional wellbeing?

Many colleges have been attempting to make their environments "Veteran friendly." We have over three hundred veterans per semester attending classes and have taken many steps to try an assist vets who pursue their education.

We have an Armed Forces Club that promotes camaraderie, hosts prominent speakers (i.e. Dr. Edward Tick), has Veterans Day ceremonies, and organizes pertinent vet oriented student activities.

We have qualified counselors to help with emotional/psychological readjustment.

We have a specialist trained to handle all the educational benefit issues that involve vets.

We have ongoing staff education pertinent to veterans.

We have a unique space or "Vet Friendly Zone" just for vets who want to interact with their peers.

We reach out to vets on family day and student orientation day.

I was a student veteran during the Viet Nam War era. My friends and I had to deal with some significant readjustment issues, but the returning vets today seem to have an entirely new and different dimension of concerns. They obviously need our understanding, guidance and support.

15
WAR HEALING CIRCLES

We have been meeting at the First Unitarian Universalist Society of Albany for a few months. As the room fills with feelings of anger, profound sadness and loss, some might wonder why we keep returning. As a volunteer from Soldier's Heart in Troy, I, and the other facilitator from the Society, return because we believe in the power of the experience—The War Healing Circle. Our support group is modeled after a centuries old Native American tradition simply called — the Talking Circle. The tradition honors the spoken word. There is no advice given, no political debates, and no counseling. It is simply a place to cleanse oneself of pain and suffering without judgment or condemnation. Our circle is composed of veterans (WW II, Viet Nam, Korea, Gulf War, Iraq, and Afghanistan), active duty military personnel, family members and supporters.

In the beginning of our group, a list of the deceased, recently killed in war, is read slowly. It is immediately apparent that this is not a made for TV movie or a docudrama. After the list is read, participants are invited to take the talking stick. This is a symbolic item that indicates that only the person holding it can speak. The listening that takes place is done more from the heart than with the ears. For many group members, the cleansing that takes place is the first step toward healing and wellness. They are courageous people facing their challenges directly and honestly.

Here are some comments from the participants:

As a Creative Therapist I am well aware of the healing power of story-telling, an ancient and universal tool, however, I was reminded again tonight how empowering and invaluable this experience can be. As we passed the talking stick at tonight's War Healing Circle, personal sharing and stories spoke directly to our hearts, offering understanding and empathy for both the family and individuals' struggles surrounding the military experience as a whole." Heidi

"Attending the War Healing Circle has given me an insight into the problems facing our Veterans which would not be possible in other ways. Listening to the veterans and families of veterans share their stories allows one, in a very direct manner, to better understand. Dave from Binghamton

"As the father of a Navy Seal, I find the War Healing Circle to be a place to listen and reflect. It is true we hear about veterans' issues and just as important, family issues too. We are all service members when one of our own is on active duty. We meet to share our stories and our responsibilities. We join in a community effort to illuminate the far reaching fingers of warfare that wind deeply and silently into our culture with the hopes that the world our children have lent to us will become a safer place." Stephen

"I just wanted to re-iterate, as a former active duty Air Force base family advocacy officer, that one of the deployed soldier's greatest fears is that his spouse and children will not be able to cope with the stress of single parenting in their absence. Also, we need to be sensitive to how it feels for a child to have Mom or

Dad serving in a combat zone and seeing/hearing about soldiers being killed daily, perhaps fearing to answer the phone or that knock on the door.

"It is a way for the community to really understand the veteran's perspective. For the veteran it is a way to develop a trusting partnership with the community. "Mike from Utica

After one evening's circle, I felt some sadness and sought a peaceful distraction. I sat near the Hudson River and as I saw the darkness, I thought of the circle a few hours earlier. It was a bad feeling until the moon reflected off the water and I could see the light.

16.
WHEN A CHAPLAIN DIES IN WAR

As I mentioned recently, my friend, army chaplain Lt. Chris Antal, generously gave permission to have his blog featured in my column.

9 October 2012 | Chris Antal

Last night I had dinner at the Goetz Dining Facility (DFAC) at Forward Operating Base (FOB) Walton, which is a short helicopter flight from Kandahar, Afghanistan. Before the meal, I raised a "near beer" (nonalcoholic) with a chaplain colleague to toast Dale Allen Goetz, the Army chaplain after whom the DFAC is named. Chaplain Goetz died in Afghanistan on August 30, 2010, not far from FOB Walton, and is the only military chaplain from the United States killed in action since 1970, when Phillip Arthur Nichols was killed in Vietnam.

I remember when I got the news that Chaplain Goetz had been killed. I was in the passenger seat of our family mini-van, my wife was driving, and our five kids were in the back. We were on our way back from a vacation in the Adirondack Mountains of New York. Shortly, I would be preparing for my first deployment to Afghanistan, which at that time seemed likely to happen sometime before spring. The notification came to my Blackberry from the Department of Defense List serve: "Captain Dale A. Goetz was killed when his vehicle was hit by a roadside bomb." The notice said nothing about Captain Goetz being Chaplain Goetz, but a quick search of his name on Google revealed a more complete story.

When I learned Dale Goetz was a chaplain, my gut tightened and I wanted to vomit. My first thought concerned my own mortality: I had not until that moment acknowledged the real risk I would face going to Afghanistan as a chaplain. The next thought was about the unit served by Chaplain Goetz -- the soldiers of the 1-66 Armored Battalion of the Fourth Infantry Division. When a soldier dies, the unit turns to their chaplain for comfort, hope and guidance. Their chaplain performs the memorial ceremony for the unit, and provides grief counseling to individuals. In the horror of war, the chaplain is a reminder to many of a loving and compassionate God who is present even amidst terrible suffering. But what does it mean when the chaplain gets killed? How do soldiers cope with the existential angst that must arise from such a tragedy -- the very angst, which in the moment I heard the news, was making me nauseous.

When the chaplain gets killed, some will face one of life's most perennial questions: why do bad things happen to good people? When the chaplain gets killed some will question the invincibility of "the armor of God" (Ephesians 6: 10-18) which fails to protect God's very own representative. When the chaplain gets killed some will face the dreadful realization that we are all vulnerable and nobody is really safe. When the chaplain gets killed -- the chaplain who is a non-combatant and carries no weapon -- some will ask where is justice? Where is fairness? When the chaplain gets killed some will examine previously held assumptions: "God is on our side," "God will protect us," "God will not let anything bad happen to us," and "In God we trust," -- and perhaps reject long held beliefs.

Yes, when the chaplain gets killed many will suffer moral injury -- defined by Jonathan Shay as "a betrayal of what is right." And sometimes a moral injury can be the most debilitating wound of war -- the wound that is most difficult to heal. To heal from moral injury we need to give meaning to tragedy which might otherwise be inherently meaningless. I have made the tragic killing of Chaplain Goetz meaningful to me by reflecting on his death, examining some of my assumptions, and correcting false views. I am glad for the simple memorial of the Goetz DFAC at FOB Walton, which reminds me of his death, and the sacrifice made by his wife, Christy, and their three sons. I thank and honor Dale Allen Goetz for helping me, in his death, move beyond self-deception towards a more right view of warfare and a greater reverence for life.

17.
EVENTS THAT SUPPORT OUR VETS

MEMORIAL DAY WEEKEND 2013

My column this week is a compilation of some of the events that I was told about or participated in recently.

On the Wednesday night before Memorial Day weekend, mom, Jackson, Kyra and I attended a meaningful ceremony at the reverend Francis A. Kelley chapter of the Disabled American Veterans in North Troy. My mother and two other WW II veterans were awarded medals that they were entitled to over sixty years ago. The two men were brothers Michael and Frank Cocca from Green Island. The organization's members did a great job at putting together the research, enduring the lengthy paper work and having the patience necessary for this event to happen.

On Thursday, I left home to attend and present at a conference called, "When Johnny Comes Marching Home ... And Gets Arrested." This get together was described as "A gathering of veterans, concerned professionals, advocates and members of the academic and general community, to discuss the state of veterans in our criminal justice system; and a call of action for reform." Since I have been volunteering, with the national organization "Soldier's Heart" based in Troy, for a few years, I was happy to be a participant. I have also written about twenty veteran oriented columns and one that was particularly relevant - "The Sentencing of a Marine" (3/15/2009). The other attendees were from all over the country and there was even a woman there from Greece. I've been to a lot of conferences during my career but I don't think that I have ever met a more diverse, intelligent, skilled and compassionate group than the one assembled last weekend.

Lauren Dunn sent me the following information.

"The Albany VA Veterans' Quilts were donated in a special ceremony to the Friends of the NYS Military Museum, Saratoga. After four years of traveling to different locations throughout the region, the Veterans' Quilts have found a permanent home. The Story of the Veterans' Quilts began in May 2009 when a team of the 15 employees and Volunteers at the Stratton VA Medical Center started the Quilting Bee of Acknowledgement project to commemorate Veterans for their service. Team members interviewed and assisted veterans, employees and their families to collect stories, pictures and memorabilia from their service years.

The team distributed kits, which included fabric squares and a form for autobiographical information regarding their service years. They initially thought that only a few kits would be returned, possibly 30 squares. In total, they received 189 squares. What started out as a single small quilt, became two 8 ft. x 10 ft. very large quilts. Most viewers are emotionally moved when seeing the vast display of quilts, which represent Veterans from as far back to the revolutionary war. Of perhaps equal impact is the accompanying book "The Quilting Bee of Acknowledgement". The book captures the biographies and pictures of each person honored on the quilt. The initial printing cost was funded by a local Devote story of the quilt can be found on the Sage website under: Veterans' Quilting Bee of Acknowledgement". I have seen the quilts at Russell Sage a few years ago. It was a wonderful, heartfelt experience.

About a year ago, I started a column entitled, "When a Chaplain Dies in War." I never finished it because the chaplain I spoke to about this story, Lt. Chris Antal, was deployed. He is back from Afghanistan and has told the story on his blog. He has given me permission to print this meaningful and sensitive piece.

My Uncle...

18.
WHAT'S REALLY IMPORTANT?

My mother handed me a letter that made me very happy. It said that, "grave 4A#3 has been reserved for Josephine Smith and grave 4A#2 has been reserved for John Ostwald, both veterans." We will be so close so that we can "hold hands under the dirt" as grandma used to say. Barring an unforeseeable accident or terminal illness in my case, she will die before me. Some parents of veterans are not so fortunate these days. They face what grandma said was "the worst thing that can happen to a human being – having their child die before them." It happens in other ways too but wars often seem preventable and often unnecessary.

Last week the media reported that a local man from River St. was killed in Iraq. A U.S. firm was accused of bilking millions in Iraq. A bomb killed thirty people. Three of them U.S. service men. A ten-year veteran refused to go back for a second tour and mentioned "scenes of misery, such as a badly burned young girl and mass graves filled with men, women and children."

What are we doing over there? Is this about freedom or money and politics? Will any of these service men and women come home unscarred? Do we feel any safer? Are we becoming captives in our own country? Are we doing any good?

We want answers. We need answers. In my angry moments when I have no answers I wonder if the government is being run by religious zealots who don't believe in judgment day.

Certainly, my perspective is the opposite of many other Americans. My friend, Charlie said, "If 9/11 taught us anything it taught us that you have to be proactive to prevent future terrorist acts." Charlie's son just went to Iraq. I wondered if his personal investment in the war might change his opinion.

Jim Margo, a retired major in the National Guard, says, "right or wrong we back our President and follow through till this war is finished and behind us." Author and activist Edward Abbey stated that "A patriot must always be ready to defend his country against his government." One of my students who returned from a tour in Iraq is not a supporter of the war. Her friend was killed and she been diagnosed with Post Traumatic Stress disorder at the age of 25.

Answers are difficult to get when we have few facts. Who is the enemy in this war? Does anyone have a fact regarding this question? During World War II, it seemed clear. I read something recently that didn't include facts yet it made a significant impression on me. It was an article in The Sun (May 2005) written by Norman Fischer, a Zen Priest, poet and author of Taking Our Places: The Buddhist Path to Truly Growing Up. Mr. Fisher doesn't seem to be a fan of the president - "a man whose idea of preserving freedom includes a full-scale invasion of a foreign nation on false pretenses" yet he offers an interesting perspective. "We should ask ourselves: Is there anything of value in what this president says? Can I in some way appreciate the views that are being advanced? And if I must oppose them, can I do so respectfully and intelligently, without feeling that I am opposing idiots and evildoers, but rather people who might have worthwhile hearts and minds of their own?"

I mentioned my column to Mom and she said, "We won't be worrying too much about this war stuff fifty years from now. All that matters is that you and I will be enjoying the beautiful view of Troy from St. Mary's cemetery.

19. VETERANS NEED MORE THAN PRAISE

Me, Chip, Ryan, and Mike were unloading a rental truck the other day at Diamond Ridge, a retirement community off Oakwood Ave. The truck was filled with over eighty years of memories along with the usual couches, tables and TV sets. What courage it must have taken for Chip's in-laws, Ed and Marie to up root their entire life in Philadelphia and move to a new land, Troy.

While we brought in the endless number of boxes, one spilled open and revealed a unique treasure. Most people wouldn't recognize it immediately. It is somewhat odd looking but stunning to those who really know what it is – the Purple Heart. It is a medal given for being wounded in action during wartime. Chip's father in law, Ed, was wounded during a combat mission in Germany. Chip and I were startled when another treasure fell out of the box- the Bronze Stared never mentioned to Chip, a former Marine Captain, that he was awarded this additional medal. The bronze star is given for acts of bravery above and beyond the call of duty.

A few months earlier, I received a letter that said, "Your medals and awards have arrived." Shortly after receiving the letter, I was at the VFW in North Greenbush with other Vets from WWII and the Viet Nam era. My kids were smiling proudly and my mother, a WW II Army vet, was beaming as I received some awards. I am certainly no hero. I was out of the country for a while and away from home for a few years. There were real war heroes at the ceremony. Men like Ed.

Some of us witnessed a touching moment when a frail elderly man with a cane was called to receive his medals from service in World War II. He rose from his seat, stood at attention and proudly walked forward without the cane. Once a soldier, always a soldier. A number politicians and civil servants spoke at this ceremony. Their words of thanks and praise were very sincere. Like some people, I assumed that they were there primarily for the photo opportunity but I was wrong.

It was a wonderful and moving ceremony yet I was on edge and felt some discomfort that I couldn't explain. A few days later the reason for my angst became clear when important questions came up for me.

When all the parades are over, the medals given out and the monuments erected will the American public really help Veterans get what they really need? Will aging Vets get adequate medical help and psychological support? Will younger vets, of the current Iraq conflict get these services and assistance with vocational readjustment, education and help for their families? I was very lucky that I was not adversely affected by the few years that I spent in the Navy during the Viet Nam conflict. I benefited by having most of my college education paid for and having a free burial plot next to my mother. Many young men and woman were not so lucky. They either gave their lives or suffer from lifelong serious impairment.

Veterans although numerous seem to have little power to influence politicians and lawmakers. We are glad to see the flag waving, patriotic singing at ball games and praising our efforts but we need your help to influence lawmakers to provide more concrete, practical ways to show some appreciation.

Congresswoman Kirsten Gillibrand, who recently toured Iraq, really clarified and summarized this issue when she said, "We need to continue the discussion in Washington that federal spending reflects our country's priorities, and there is no higher priority than the health and well-being of our veterans and the men and women in the Armed Forces. Our country's veterans, members of the Armed Services and their families have answered the call to serve our country, and it is critical that we provide them with the proper benefits that they deserve."

20.
ONE NEVER GETS OVER A BIG LOSS

About 1990, I returned to Troy from living in New York City and recall unpacking pictures of mom, dad and Uncle Sonny. They were all World War II vets. So were uncles Paul and Marco but I didn't have their pictures. Dad and Uncle Paul died within the last five years in their seventies. Uncle Sonny died when he was nineteen in 1941.The last picture that I unpacked was mine. It was comical when compared to the black and white pictures of the past. I was supposed to look like a virile vet but looked more like a prepubescent, female cheerleader because of all the color touch ups. You know what I mean. Look at a family photo taken at a studio.

My mind wandered, as I looked over the photos, and I was thinking that some of these people had seen horrors in World War II that most of us can only imagine or see in films. It is the same for most wars – carnage, atrocities on both sides, immorality and insanity. The psycho emotional causalities of war live on long after the actual violence has ended. The October 1944 issue of the magazine, Ladies Home Companion, called it "psychoneurosis." Words like shell-shocked and combat fatigue have also attempted to describe this tragic mental state. The more current recognizable diagnostic label is Post Traumatic Stress Disorder. The phrase is seen often in the modern media probably because it can be used when discussing many traumas like sexual abuse or even natural disasters.

Unfortunately, three men that I know well have been consumed by this disorder. One was probably my best friend as a preteen. One was an acquaintance in the neighborhood who was a little older than I. Finally, the third man and I became close friends shortly after the war in the seventies. All three have been tortured by the demons presented graphically in nightmares and flashbacks. All three have had serious problems with chemical dependency. One had a criminal experience followed by lengthy incarceration.

Aggression, isolation, and hyper vigilance are also usual symptoms.

After about twenty-five years of torment and chaos, two of these men have risen from their own ashes like the mythical phoenix. Psychotherapeutic interventions have assisted them in their quest to return to a somewhat normal life. Their courage and resiliency amaze me because I had seen them during some of their desperate hours. My third friend, who I have not seen for some time, is still lost in the haze of alcohol, depression and despair. If you have God's ear, please whisper a prayer for our friend and comrade before he is truly lost.

Like many of you, I am often confused about decisions to wage war. We are angry and want to fight when someone tries to hurt us. We are arrogant and think, "How dare they attack us?" Whether it is economics, politics, anger or arrogance we are certainly not fully aware of the real damage of war that lasts for years after the last veteran comes home. Within the past two years when we went into Afghanistan and Iraq, I asked myself two simple questions. "Will my children be safer? And "Is this doing any good?" I came up with the wrong answers.

The only thing that is clear to me about war is this. I miss my 19-year-old uncle who died in 1941 before I was born. During my life, I have imagined him as a mentor, guide and lifelong friend. As I weep, I know that I am like a child who grieves for love lost. This is why I hate war.

A COMRADE IN ARMS
KNOWN BUT TO GOD

21.
VETERANS PART I

I naively wondered why Mouse's picture was on the front page of the paper. I hadn't seen him since he left for Vietnam. The first word that I saw under his name was "wounds" and I felt strangely relieved until I saw the second word, "fatal " then I cried.

His real name was Michael O'Connor. He was a local guy that played pool and cards with us. He was harmless, quiet and sometimes funny. He was just Mouse. The bright red, white and blue colors that blanketed his coffin and the 8x10 of him in his uniform were my last memories. A short time later, my friend Bobby and I left from the Rensselaer train station for boot camp in the Great Lakes.

It was such an odd time for young men especially with draft cards, draft physicals and the intimidating draft lottery - an unpopular war in a chaotic time. The Kent State tragedy, which resulted in the deaths of four students by the action of the National Guard, seemed to highlight this confusion and divisiveness. At one point, our base in the Great Lakes was on high alert because of the threats of violent demonstrations following Kent State. I was also reminded again of the unpopularity of the war when I hitchhiked from Norfolk, Va. to Troy in my uniform. It took me a while to get a ride. If it was the World War II era, I might have been offered a ride all the way home, plus money and food. It was a different ballgame then.

Even though I would be on active duty in the Navy, and less likely to be in combat than the Marines or Army, I was still scared. My fears intensified when I received orders for a unit called Inshore Undersea Warfare Group Two. We were lucky. Our unit trained for a couple years, traveled a little and most of us came home when the war was winding down in the early seventies. Guantanamo Bay was our last stop and I finally realized that our training would not be utilized in "Nam." I have endless stories and anecdotes about this period in my life and it might sound corny but I am convinced that the service helped to "straighten me out." I am proud to be a veteran.

In 1985, I was hiking around the out skirts of Maastricht, Holland when I saw a beautiful 30-foot angel with wings expanded. She was hovering over a small pond. It turned out to be a statue at the entrance to a cemetery. I remember thinking, "What a beautiful country and what lovely cemeteries these people have for themselves. "I walked through and read some of the names. They were not Dutch names. Rows, and rows and rows of American names on chaste, white stones. The Dutch people were showing their gratitude for World War II vets with this magnificent monument to eternal sacrifice. I never thought about this simple idea before. There must be millions of people outside of the United States who were saved by the actions our armed forces and who show their gratitude in ways we may never see or know about.

Later that week I was riding with friends on one of those German highways where you can go over 100 miles an hour. I forget what it is called. The name of a

German town jumped out of a row of trees seconds later – Dachau. We stopped at the site of the infamous concentration camp and entered the actual grounds where torture, despair, and death were the norm. I had no personal connection with this place but I felt something indescribable and ominous. It is the feeling that people who visit Ground Zero will have even decades from now. There is something inside of us that senses when something horrible has happened.

PEACE

22.
I'M PROUD TO BE AN AMERICAN

I was invited by my friend, Ed Tick, to March in the Memorial Day parade in Albany. I don't do parades but I like to watch them with my WW II Army veteran mom, Josephine. I marched enough when I was in the service. I changed my mind when he said that I could march with the group, "Veterans for Peace. "We would be marching not just for the recognition for being veterans but also for a meaningful cause – to seek peace. I brought my son Jackson with me to keep him busy for the morning, to teach him more about war/peace and to give him some exercise. I let him wear my dad's VFW club hat and one of the marchers gave him a peace flag.

After I parked the car, I spotted the group who were holding various flags and banners with peace related messages. There was one gentleman that I noticed right away. He was probably in his late seventies or older. He wore a full dress uniform. I also noticed a desert storm Marine who easily could have been mistaken for a civilian protester from the sixties. Before I went over to the group, I chatted with one of the members of a biker's organization that sounded like "patriots for …; I can't remember the name. We shared pertinent veteran backgrounds and talked about the march. In the middle of our conversation, he said something like, "my wife told me to stay away from those protesters." He pointed to our group. I said proudly, "That's who I'm with. " He immediately stopped talking and walked away. I was confused. We veterans and supporters are advocating pursuing Peace versus War. The kids would say, "It's a no brainer!" I asked Dan Wilcox, the vice-president of the Tom Paine Chapter (#10) Veterans for Peace about the mission of the organization so I could get some clarity. He said, "We draw on our personal experiences and perspectives gained as veterans to raise public awareness of the true costs and consequences of militarism and war - and to seek peaceful, effective alternatives. "This sounded fine to me. On with the parade!

Jackson loved all the attention and was given a bunch of peace necklaces to pass out to the parade watchers. I felt proud carrying the veterans for Peace flag alongside of Old Glory. Many of the watchers applauded, some looked quizzically and only one person expressed disgust overtly. She was a middle-aged woman who stared and gave us the thumbs down sign. I got a little angry because it seemed like she was glaring at my naive nine year old. I asked Jackson about this gesture and he said, "Why does she want people to die?" I came up with some ambiguous explanation and he shook his head.

Near the end of the parade, I noticed the sweat coming from under the hat and onto the cheeks of the elderly vet who wore the heavy cloth uniform while carrying a banner. My admiration for him soared. This man, despite the heat and fatigue was actively demonstrating for a cause that he believed in. This is what makes me proud to be an American.

23.
Boot Camp Memories

As we approach the Memorial Day holiday, I thought that I would share memories from some veterans about their first contact with the Armed Forces – basic training.

Ken - Marines

"One day in boot camp in 1963 in California, the drill Instructor was away so I thought I would imitate him. I got up on a bench and yelled at the guys like he did many times before. He would put his arms at his side and bark like a dog at us. Well, I did not know that he was right around the corner and was watching the whole thing. I got in all kinds of trouble but he had a smile on his face and said, "Ken you had me down perfect but I have to punish you for this." "So in the sand box I go doing pushups until I couldn't breathe. That's the Marine Corps for you."

Frank-Navy

"Going to boot camp was certainly high anxiety since it was the first time I was really away from home alone. You don't know what to expect. First, you are introduced to your drill instructor who is the most intimidating individual you will ever meet! You learn quick lessons on listening, responding and keeping your mouth shut. Punishment is harsh but upon reflection it was part of the structure and discipline I sorely needed at the time."

Steve– Air Force

"While I thought that USAF basic training was a colossal waste of time and energy, I did learn something important about the social world I live in. Growing up in the California suburbs of the 1950s, the ethnic world to me was whites. I knew no African Americans and probably had never spoken to one though I was aware of the Civil Rights Movement and had a vague understanding of the early-1960s racial situation in the South. In basic training, for the first time, I worked with and lived under the same barracks roof as scores of African Americans from the south. They were a lot like me but with one important exception. I joined because a friend of mine from high school did and he said that he worked an 8-5 job and received a college education for free. The African American men I knew joined to get out of the South. I saw a college education as my ticket to success in life; they saw anyplace but the South as theirs."

Christine - Army Nurse Corps

"I received a Direct Commission into the Army Medical Command as an Army Reserve Nurse Corps Officer and because of this status had an abbreviated AMEDD Basic Course where they introduced us to some basic soldier skills. What I can share is that the comrades I lived and worked with during those times have become true friends. Thirty plus years later, we still all get together every few months and have shared our lives with each other through the good times and the hard times. Finding these lifelong friends was one of the greatest experiences of joining the military."

Me - Navy

“My buddy and I left home in upstate New York on a train that was heading for the Great Lakes Training Center near Chicago. We were young and anxious. My buddy's sea bag was filled with cans of beer. When we got to the base, he was blind drunk. We met guys from all over the country. It was a great learning experience. When you told these guys you were from New York, they all thought it was either the Bronx or Brooklyn not upstate. Some guy asked me if I normally carried a knife.”

“The drill instructor abused us regularly then told us to write a nice letters to our mothers. I forgot how many weeks boot camp lasted but today I realize that it helped me develop the internal strength that I needed to get through some difficult challenges in life."

Each basic training experience has a different personality that is shaped by the disposition of the drill instructor, branch of the service, time period and even climate. Some of my students ask me for advice before they go to boot camp. I always say the same thing. "Keep quiet, don't joke around, don't ask questions and do whatever they say."

PARIS.FR
1

24.
Korea: The Forgotten War

I got the folding chairs out of the garage and prepared for our annual ritual. Mom picked me up to drive us to the Memorial Day parade. I know what you are thinking, "Why is mom picking me up and not the other way around?" I don't know. She is ninety and independent and unpredictable.

The parade was long and terrific but I noticed something that struck me as unusual. In the middle of the Humvee, marching bands, and fire trucks, there was a car pulling a small trailer with three men in it who were probably in their mid-eighties. It wasn't the men or their transport that caught my attention but the banner on the vehicle that shouted, "Korea: the Forgotten War." They were right. These men and many others like them have been forgotten, like the war was, and neglected by our country.

My curiosity led me to the internet for some relevant information and also to the home of Larry Novak, a Korean War veteran. First, some historical background. According to Wikipedia, The Korean War was a war between North and South Korea, in which a United Nations force led by the United States of America fought for the South, and China fought for the North, which was also assisted by the Soviet Union. The war arose from the division of Korea at the end of World War II and from the global tensions of the Cold War that developed immediately afterwards. In August 1950, the President and the Secretary of State obtained the consent of Congress to appropriate $12 billion for military action in Korea. The war ended in 1953. Data from the U.S. Department of Defense indicated that the United States suffered 33,686 battle deaths, along with 2,830 non-battle deaths, during the Korean War. In contrast, it is estimated that there were 58,220 casualties during the Viet Nam conflict.

After my internet search, I met with Larry. Even before I spoke to him, at his home, I could sense his passion. Over the phone, he made the dramatic statement, "It was a police action." He wasn't talking about the current racial conflicts and violence involving police but about what historians often refer to as "the hidden war." He followed with, "It was President Truman's fault!" When we spoke privately, in person, I was able to get a better understanding of his angry comment.

First, I asked him about President Truman's statement. Larry said that he and other vets were denied benefits because their conflict was called a "Police Action" by the president. I didn't clearly understand this issue so I looked on the VA hospital's website and it seems like they serve almost all veterans. I called Larry for clarification and he said that things were better now, but immediately after the Korean War, "Those that really needed help couldn't get it."

Larry vividly described his career in the Navy from 1951-1953. He remembered the names of the ships and especially the "Diphda", a supply ship that was named after the bright giant star in the constellation Cetus. He also described at length the many trips back and forth from the United States to Korea.

I have interviewed veterans of other wars before and most often, they have something unique to say while they tell me the comprehensive story of their service. Larry had a unique experience that surpassed most of the others. He was on the USS Sarsi when it struck a mine and sank off the coast of North Korea in August of 1952.Larry and the other survivors spent the night clinging to life rafts, life preservers and the ship's whaleboat. Larry's description of this event was filled with strong emotional reactions even now sixty-three years later.

Our interview was win/win. I believe that Larry had a cathartic pleasurable experience while telling his story and I learned more about a great guy and the confusing "Police Action" that lasted over three years.

25.
A DRY POST

It is as rare as a unicorn, dodo bird or a phoenix. It is a dry (no alcohol) armed forces Post. Alcohol used by veterans is a social vehicle but also the curse of many vets recovering from especially the traumas of war and deployment. My best friend, from my childhood, drank himself to death in a local Post.

A local veteran, that I've met a few times, has taken the initiative to provide an alcohol free environment where vets can still share armed forces experiences and enjoy the social aspects of being with their comrades. His name is Robert Porter and this is his story.

"I served in the US Marine Corps from 1986 to 2007.I was a Military Policeman), Criminal Investigator, a Drill Instructor and Military Police Instructor. I was also trained as a Substance Abuse Control Officer and it was my job to work with Marines who either asked for help with alcohol issues or were identified by someone as having an alcohol problem. Even though I was trained and knew what the pitfalls of alcohol where, I was arrested for drunk driving in 2003."

"After returning from a combat tour in Iraq, where I trained Iraqi Police, and retiring in 2007, I realized drinking was not good for my new life as a civilian. I didn't join Alcoholics Anonymous .I wasn't an alcoholic but still abused alcohol all those years. Part of my transition was to become a member of our Veterans Originations: American Legion, Disabled American Veterans (DAV), Marine Corps League (MCL), Veterans of Foreign Wars (VFW) and an all Marine Motorcycle Club called the Leathernecks."

"The unifying factor of all these Veterans Organizations was once again Alcohol! The Posts where they held their meetings and events served "inexpensive" alcohol to the members. The image the VFW is trying to change is of a dark, smoke filled bar with old Veterans drinking! I saw the problem that had been in the Military being continued into the civilian world and I didn't like it. As a new member and not an Officer of any of the organizations, there was little I could do. I was fortunate to meet some Veterans who thought as I did, some of them were in AA, but not all. However, we were the minority and nothing changed."

"Recently, some of us moved to the Louis W Oppenheim VFW Post 1019, at 481 Washington Ave, Albany, NY 12206. During my first meeting at the Oppenheim, I was voted the Junior Vice Commander. The Post had decided not to renew its Liquor license in 2010, due to declining member attendance and participation. The Post had financial problems so over the next several months I worked on keeping it open and getting the DAV to hold meetings there. I also got American Bikers Aimed Towards Education (ABATE) of New York, Inc. to hold their state meetings at the Post."

"I looked into boosting the member attendance and participation, and saw the other VFW's all offered alcohol, so renewing our liquor license wouldn't draw any new members. So, I decided to keep the Post "DRY" and transform it into a "Starbucks" type establishment. Eventually, we'd get rid of all the pool tables and "Bar" accoutrements and replaced them with lounge chairs and sofas. Bring in Wi-Fi and even offer video game tournaments as an activity. To add to this, I worked with different people, some of whom were Veterans in AA, to get meetings at the Post."

"Now, I'm the Commander in charge of the Post; the Coffee Canteen is open from 6 to 10 pm every Saturday night. We also have AA meetings every Saturday night at 7pm. There are DAV and ABATE of NY Inc. meetings once a month. We are getting new members, many of who are Iraq and Afghanistan veterans from local colleges. So the Post is being revitalized and will shine again!"

Robert is encountering some resistance to this meaningful endeavor but it is hoped that his Post will thrive and offer vets a needed change in the military culture.

04/12/2004

26.
Veterans' Justice

During the past few years, I have written more than 25 columns on veterans' issues. Included were topics like Veterans on Campus, the Patriot Flight, PTSD, Journeys of Reconciliation to Vietnam, and the War Healing Circles. The one I am presenting to you today may be the most provocative and most important of all of them.

The information below has evolved out the work of an organization called "It Could Happen To You (ITCHY)." Their current efforts involve lobbying for a bills related to the legal process called "discovery." The discovery stage in legal proceedings is defined as "the entire efforts of a party to a lawsuit and his/her/its attorneys to obtain information before trial through demands for production of documents, depositions of parties and potential witnesses, written interrogatories (questions and answers written under oath), written requests for admissions of fact, examination of the scene and the petitions and motions employed to enforce discovery rights. The theory of broad rights of discovery is that all parties will go to trial with as much knowledge as possible and that neither party should be able to keep secrets from the other (except for constitutional protection against self-incrimination).

Basically, this process in New York seems to be replete with chicanery, wrongdoing and deception. The harm caused by these practices is profound. People have been arrested, imprisoned and even given the death penalty unjustly. The specific implications for veterans, who have interacted in combat zones, related to discovery are also extremely important.

Some of the situations that are relevant to veterans are supplied below by Jonathan E. Gradess, executive director of the New York State Defenders Association (NYSDA). Gradess pointed out: "The following "carryover" behaviors — red flags suppressed in discovery — are things that might appear in a police report that could give rise to letting a lawyer for the defense know that he is handling a case affected by the client's combat experience and military service."

For example, the following behaviors of simply driving a motor vehicle have been documented as modification resulting from combat duty:

• Driving at excessive speeds in the center lane (thus avoiding ambush or roadside bombs);

• Speeding up at intersections (to avoid gunfire);

• Speeding and weaving in and out of traffic (trained safe driving tactics in combat);

• Weapons within reach in a vehicle;

• A driver being "lost" or having no recognition of being somewhere where they would otherwise be familiar with;

• Hyper vigilance;

• Easily startled by noises;

• Avoiding overpasses and bridges;

• Tracking/scanning for objects while driving resulting in distracted driving;

• Avoiding certain color/size vehicles, avoiding vehicles driving next to them;

• Unwilling to pull over when requested by police agency;

• Out of proportion aggressiveness;

• Unwillingness to provide information or purposely limiting information given to police personnel;

• Instant anger/rage if someone touches their belongings within vehicle;

• Refusing to wear seat belts, so they can exit vehicle quickly;

• Avoiding driving by roadside construction crews or reducing speed in construction sites; and

• Doesn't stop for traffic, pedestrians, always has the right of way.

As I read these items for the first time, I recalled working with a few student vets who consistently mentioned how their war experiences influenced driving in our non-combat traffic situations. It was disconcerting to hear how much anxiety they had.

Gradess also supplied some other insights. Service member's accidents increase about 13 percent after deployment, according to studies. Binghamton, New York actually has a driving class for recently returned veterans called "Returning Warrior 10 Miler."

Gradess noted that that tweaking the existing judicial process could play a role in helping veterans.

"Discovery in New York is scant, particularly so with police reports where information turned over to both prosecution and defense should happen simultaneously," Gradess said. "With veterans such reports represent a virtual gold mine of information that could inform a capable defense attorney of the special status of a veteran client."

The specific state bill related to all of the information above is the Justice for Our Veterans Act.

27.
Who Are Vets - They All Touch Our Lives

As Veterans' day approaches, a simple question comes to mind. Who are veterans? I asked a few local people what they think of when they hear the word.

"When I hear the word "veteran" I immediately think of the veterans of World War II. I read about the war, especially the battles in Italy, where my parents grew up and barely survived the war as teenagers, I am always extremely appreciative of the sacrifices that their generation made in order for our nation and the world to prosper." Fred Aliberti

"With the ever shrinking number of the population involved in the defense of our country, it's easy to completely forget about the enormous and vital contribution veterans have made in the history of the USA. Yet without that contribution, we'd be a very different country, if we still existed at all. We owe an enormous debt to those who have sacrificed for us; a debt we can never fully repay, which makes it all the more imperative to do all we can to show that gratitude in any way we are able." Paul Dellio

"When I hear the word veteran I think of one story. My grandfather was playing cards with his best friend on his ship, the SS Tunney, and went to get a cup of coffee, when the ship was hit by a kamikaze, and his friend was killed." Kyra TePaske

"They are people in general, not just those who served in war. They are people in any profession who have significant skills that they can pass on to others." Michael L.

"When I think of a veteran what first comes to mind is a young man in his early twenties - I envision a clean cut young adult who has entered the military to serve his country and to fight for the freedoms of America and to keep our country safe in these difficult political times - I also envision a young adult who is trying to create an identity and gain a sense of esteem. The military offers the structure and discipline to move forward in one's life. I also see their vulnerability and question the political decisions of our leaders in sending our children into war." anonymous female college professor

Veterans are a very diverse group of men and women from various branches of the armed forces. Some have been in combat. Other veterans, who have not experienced the horrors of war, still have sacrificed years away from home and loved ones. Sometime it is just luck. You can get orders for Germany, Hawaii or Afghanistan. My mother and father were WW II vets who never left the United States. My unit in the Navy was Inshore Undersea Warfare Group II based in Little Creek Va. My orders took me as far as Guantanamo Bay, Cuba.

Some veterans are wounded souls who continue to suppress their emotional pain with alcohol or other drugs. Some commit crimes and spend time incarcerated. Two of my friends spent time in State and Federal prisons. At a recent screening of the magnificent documentary, "Debt of Honor", one of the panelist mentioned that one vet completes suicide every twenty minutes. The psychological wounds seem to be much more prevalent than the physical ones. Yes, many still carry the soul wounds and seem lost. There is abundant help for veterans who have suffered from these soul wounds. Too often veterans do not seek this assistance and continue a downward spiral.

Many veterans have significant skills that are often useful in civilian life. Veteran workers are most often responsible, focused and disciplined and area a significant benefit to employers.

Although we will always be somewhat different from or civilian families, friends and neighbors; we will forever be an intimate part of the fabric of the American culture.

28.
A Serviceman's First Veterans Day - Don't Just Thank; Be Thankful

I am often asked how I decide on topics for my columns. My response is always the same; "Whatever topic I feel passionate about during the week." As you might imagine it could be anything. I decided to put aside the column that I had planned to submit when I got an email from a student veteran, Stephen Onley. He is a young man I have met only once or twice but his focus on academics, maturity at a young age and reverence for his military service impressed me. The email below describes his thoughts and feelings about Veteran's Day this past Wednesday. He gave it the title, "Don't Just Thank, Be Thankful"

"What a great morning! It's Veteran's Day!" I thought to myself as I woke up to the pattering of raindrops against my window. But this was not just any Veteran's Day. This is my first Veteran's Day since I was discharged from the military. My plans for the day consisted of attending a Flag Raising Ceremony at my college, donating a few toys to Toys for Tots, and then classes all day. As I got ready for the day, I noticed the rain was only coming down harder. A fellow student veteran sent me a text, "Are we still having the flag ceremony today?" My initial response was "If it ain't raining, then it ain't training". Maybe this is just the military mindset, but I love the rain. To be more precise, I love to be out in the rain. I never even questioned the possibility of cancelling the ceremony. But I replied, "I will be there".

After I parked my car at school, I began to walk over to the flagpole. As I made my way around the long, two-storied building between the parking lot and the flag, I saw a hand full of people standing with umbrellas. "At least somebody showed up" I thought to myself. But as I made my way around the building, I was pleasantly surprised to see a much larger group waiting for the ceremony to begin. I expected to see some of the other Student Veterans here, but this group was largely comprised of our student peers. It meant a lot to me that these young men and women of about 18 years old sacrificed a few moments in the cold rain to show their appreciation for the veterans who fought for our country. At this moment, I began to think about the people I served with during my enlistment. This led me to remember my friends, who didn't come back from Afghanistan alive.

"Thank you for your service" is what I have already heard about 50 times today. I am so thankful, that the men and women of the greatest country on the planet truly appreciate the sacrifices that I made. But this phrase is just a momentary gesture of appreciation to the servicemen and servicewomen, who are still with us today. What about those who made the ultimate sacrifice? How do we thank them? I think the words of the late President John F. Kennedy answer my question; "As we express our gratitude, we must never forget that the highest appreciation is not to utter words but to live by them."

I highly recommend that after you thank a Veteran today, or any day, think about how the service and sacrifice of these brave men and women allowed you to be where you are today. Don't just say thank you, be thankful. This is how you honor those, who have given their life so that you can have the freedoms that we all occasionally take for granted.

I am so proud to be an American.

"In memory of GYSGT Robert L. Gilbert III, USMC"

29.
Moral Dilemmas

Should I go to Greece to rest and learn or stay home to continue to support my cousin who was very ill. For some this looks like a "no brainer." Most of you would probably say, "Stay home and support your family." I went to Greece for a brief period. Here was my reasoning. I was fried and knew it. I have mentioned a few major stressors in recent columns. A national trauma expert said that I needed a "rest." I learned a long time ago that you can't be an effective helper if you are not healthy yourself. The trip was not your usual tourist trip as I mentioned in a previous column; it was designed to help the participants (mostly psychotherapists) to learn more about alternative ways to heal trauma. I knew that I would return immediately from the eleven day trip if my cousin, who had a prolonged illness, got worse quickly – he did. After four days in Greece, I got on a bus to the airport at 1:30 am, caught a plane to JFK at 6 am and drove home to Troy after I picked up my car about 3:30 pm. I got home about 7 pm. My cousin died two days later.

I mention my "moral dilemma" because as we approach Veteran's Day on November 11th, I am reminded of the extremely more complex and gut wrenching situations that arise, especially in combat zones, for our servicemen and women. I had a student some years ago who confided that he was a sniper like the one in the recent movie. He explained that he was tortured by one memory during his tour overseas. He said that he saw a kid about 13 that "didn't have a whisker on his face" point what looked like a weapon at some soldiers. A second later he fired at the child. Even though he perceived an imminent threat to his comrades, he still regretted the action and said to me solemnly, "I killed a kid."

I am familiar with a young Lieutenant's story involving calling in an air strike on a small village in Viet Nam because it was assumed that there was a strong enemy presence there. The young officer, in his twenties, vividly described seeing young children on fire screaming in pain while fleeing their homes. He said that it was his duty and he was given an order but it has been a source of remorse for years.

A marine vet in his late twenties told me about a moral dilemma he faced related to telling the truth about his service. He said he had extensive training and traveled over half the world but was never near any real combat. He had not seen or experienced some of the tragedies that his "brothers" had experienced. When he returned home, well-meaning strangers and some relatives assumed he had experienced the horrors of war at some point. His dilemma involved telling the truth, that although he was a virile capable combatant, he had not experienced the more violent aspects of war versus telling a falsehood about combat experience. Although a lie would have elevated him to a higher status in the eyes of some of the questioners, the brave young marine told the truth.

Recently, the film "The Good Kill" with Ethan Hawk highlighted the moral issues confronting pilots of an **unmanned aerial vehicle** (**UAV**), commonly known as a **drone.** The film summary states that "The targets themselves are increasingly morally ambiguous……..collateral damage goes from being a rare occurrence to a routine one. "

Please keep some of these issues in mind when welcoming our veterans home. Some may be troubled by what they did, what they saw, or what they didn't do.

HEADQUARTERS
COMPANY

U.S.ARMY

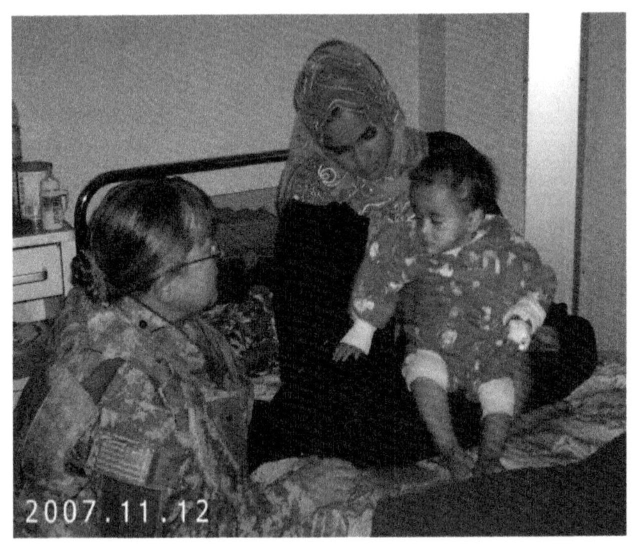
2007.11.12

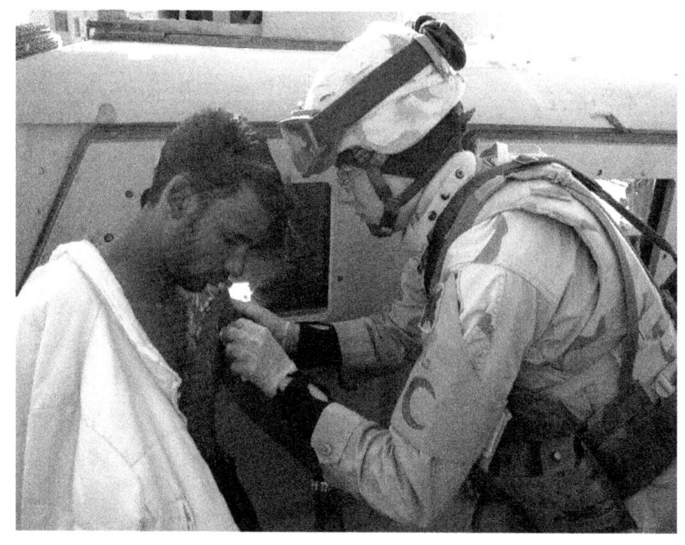

U.S.MARINES

GOEBEL
U.S. ARMY

ONE WAY
HOW IS THE
WAR ECONOMY
WORKING FOR YOU?
VETERANS FOR PEACE

ZUND-ZA
BAR
MORE
WAR
BONDS

LỄ KHANH THANH NHA ĐE XE GIA ĐINH 5
DEDICATION CEREMONY OF THE GARAGE OF FAMILY 5
trai tim nhân ai Soldier's Heart
24.10.2008

The Best Job I Ever Had

Stephen M. Kuehn

I had the privilege of being part of a specialty platoon in the 3rd United States Infantry Regiment (The Old Guard) at Fort Myer, Virginia from 2002-2008. The unit's mission is to conduct ceremonies, specifically funerals and memorial services, in Arlington National Cemetery and Washington, D.C. I began my service as a casket bearer in B Company, was eventually promoted to Sergeant, Squad Leader, and Full Honor Casket Team Leader. During a time of war in a deployable infantry company, I was primarily trained in the technical skills required to conduct funerals. In these circumstances, I became an effective leader who managed his squad, effectively communicated missions and schedules to his Soldiers, rewarded and punished them fairly, and made himself available if they had special concerns or needed assistance with personal matters.

In this essay, I intend to recognize a conflict with which I struggled. By 2007, I was an Infantry Staff Sergeant with one combat deployment (but no Combat Infantryman's Badge), the Assistant Sergeant of the Guard at the Tomb of the Unknown Soldier in charge of that platoon's operations and training programs, and starting down the pipeline for promotion to Sergeant First Class.

In 2002, my first platoon sergeant, a Gulf War veteran with 20 years' service, had taught at every level of Army institutional learning. All thirty-six of us would have confidently followed him into battle. I was not that man. I could lead, but not in combat, and I dreaded the thought that someday I would be a platoon sergeant in an infantry company on a combat deployment. I was not trained to take this next step. I was on track to become a mediocre senior NCO who could ride a staff duty desk, make the greatest PowerPoint presentations ever, and wow the chain of command with my operations orders.

I loved being a Staff Sergeant, and would have continued working as a Sentinel at the Tomb of the Unknown Soldier for the remainder of my career. But that was not possible. I felt it necessary to leave the best job I have ever had. I had no choice once I recognized where my potential would lead. And so.... I became an Officer. Looking back, that statement seems laughable, as only a veteran might understand. I knew I had more to offer the Army and had goals beyond retiring as an NCO. Crossing over "to the dark side" allowed me to apply my leadership abilities and limited Infantry skills to the Medical Service Corps. I was retrained in organizational leadership and tactics and quickly became proficient at current combat procedures. At first, I was a dumb Lieutenant, just like the other dumb Lieutenants in my brigade, and as such, my Soldiers and leaders understood that I needed to learn and gain experience in order to become a good Lieutenant. In contrast, if I had been a Sergeant First Class in an infantry unit, I would have been expected to execute operations beyond my capabilities.

My choice was a good one. I conducted combat operations in Afghanistan and after nine months brought all my soldiers home. I have since left the Army without regret and with some measure of pride. I wonder, however, what happens to others who find themselves in circumstances similar to mine. As well, I can only imagine what happens to good soldiers who are not fulfilled by their military experience. Who do not bring all their Soldiers home. Who, due to illness, injury, bad behavior, downsizing, or mission changes, do not complete their tours. Who do not deploy during a time of war. If their friends are killed in combat…? Who enter a civilian job with regrets about leaving the military, a job they loved, even when they hated it. A job not to be found in the private sector.

Similarly, many veterans find themselves unable to move forward because civilian life fails to provide the sense of fulfillment found in military service. They define personal achievement in the context of what has passed and critique the present and future against idealized memories. Many view their service as a positive and defining moment. But others see it as the time they most regret. They can neither undo nor re-do the things which haunt them. Neither can they find a comparable civilian experience that will satisfy their longing to try again? I wonder if I would have felt the same had I separated before deciding to pursue a commission.

I am fortunate that I do not regret the decisions I made as I progressed through and eventually ended my military career. I am currently enrolled in medical school and have met and become engaged to the love of my life. In other words, I have found civilian life fulfilling. The military, however, remains an integral part of who I am, and I have entered the National Guard. Not as a result of nostalgia, however, but as both a source of financial support and an ongoing opportunity to actively help soldiers who need someone who understands the effects of their unique lifestyle upon their physical and mental health. I trust that I am still able to do the things that have made the memories of my military service so wonderful. By so doing, I may find it possible to make even better memories in the future.

A returned soldier from Iraq finds himself both enlightened and confused by the American presence there yet even more so by the ignorance of those who have not served - individuals that another veteran of another war chooses to term "citizens." In country, a little girl, her father missing, her brother dead, presses into his hand a necklace. When asked what the charm means, she replies, "Allah." The narrator can never again be the same.

In an American bar, another drinker, a citizen, begins carrying on about "Muslamic radicals," and the narrator responds violently.

He has become one of "Them."

Them

Ryan Smithson

People talk to me about "towel heads" and "terrorists." It's always "us" versus "them." And how are *we* right and how are *they* wrong? People throw this shit in my face because they want it to be validated. Because they think I share their sentiments. Because I'm an Iraq War veteran, and how else would I feel?

Truth is, I did. I hated those people. *Hajis*, that's what we called 'em. *Fuckin' hajis*. We tried to be nice to 'em. We tried to level with 'em, tried to get a good picture of who they are and what they wanted. And they'd betray us. They'd sell us out to the highest bidder in town and then act as double agents. Fuck! Lost good men to tricks like that. So yeah, I hated *haji*. Wanted to kill every last one.

But you spend enough time on the ground in Iraq and you get to know 'em. You still hate 'em, sure, cause you know you can't trust 'em. But you *know* them. You get their culture and their perception. You understand 'em. And you start to learn how ass backwards your own culture is. America. We're the "us." Well, let me tell you, on the other side of the planet, we're the "them."

A guy pops a squat next to me in a bar. I mention that I served in Iraq. Don't usually tell people that. People don't get it. They don't want to understand and I don't want to explain. So I keep it to myself. But, tonight, I've had a few and my tongue's loose. Shoulda seen his eyes light up. Like he just met Neil fuckin' Armstrong. Hey pal, I didn't walk on the moon. I just rode around the desert in a Humvee. But he won't hear it. I'm a hero to this guy, a hero who, he assumes, is as much of a bigot as himself.

So he starts rantin' and ravin' about "these fuckin' insurgents" and "who do they think they are" and "if they got a problem with his country, they should meet him, one-on-one at Ground Zero and fight like men." Can you believe it? *His* country. He actually said that. Like he ever fought for her. And all this time while he's carryin' on about Muslamic radicalists (his words), I'm thinking about this little girl.

She can't be more than nine years old, crouched under a window in her mud-and-bricks home afraid because insurgents have come to her village and are terrorizing the people again. Last week, she watched her older brother bleed to death, stabbed because he wouldn't join their ranks. Her father's been missing since he swore vengeance for his son. We found his body this morning, desecrated and burnt in an alleyway, but I don't tell this little girl that. Now it's just her and her mother, barely getting by. Well, the US cavalry has rolled into town, ladies. My job is to stay with these two broads as my squad kicks down doors looking for the bad guys who won't stop blowing shit up.

And while we sit underneath the window, her mother praying quietly in the corner, this little girl reaches into her pocket and pulls out a gold necklace. It has a charm, an Arabic character, but I can't tell what it says. She looks up at me with these large, brown eyes, takes my hand in hers and places the necklace in it.

"What's it say?" I ask.

"Allah," she says, smiling.

I glance around their tiny house. A few dishes lie here and there. Some old prayer rugs. There's a wooden table and chairs which she tells me her father made. There's some old pots and a stove which barely works. What little food they have sits in a hotel-size refrigerator, and a shelf holds a few books, the only one that's clean at all being a copy of the Koran. This necklace is the only thing with any value, and it sits in *my* hand. Now I know it's an insult to refuse a gift in this culture. But I say, "no" anyway. She smiles, this nine-year-old, and shakes her head. She puts it around my neck and clasps it.

"Yours," she says. "Yours."

I say the only thing I can say, "Shukran"—thank you—one of the few words I actually know in Arabic.

Well we bagged those sons o' bitches that were terrorizing that village, and we sent the survivors down to Abu Ghraib. And that little girl and her mother are alive today because of the god-forsaken US cavalry.

AND THEN, NINE months after I come home, that little girl's charm still hangin' around my neck, I get this drunken cowboy in a bar in Brooklyn who opens his mouth and lets fall out all the filth that composes him. He's yellin' about "hajis" like he actually knows what that word means. He's screamin' about "the liberals who are as much an enemy to freedom as terrorists." He's ramblin' about *them*: Al-qaeda and the

Tally-Ban. He's got the whole crowd going and he's goin' on and on about "preserving freedom" and all that other bullshit George W. rhetoric that got us into this mess in the first place.

And all I can think of is that little girl crouchin' under a window, scared to death for her daddy, knowing more about freedom at nine years old than this drunken asshole ever will.

So when my hand leaves its position on my glass of Johnnie Walker and clenches into a fist, I don't regret it. When that fist slices through the air like a missile toward this cowboy's face, I don't regret it. When my knuckles make contact, and I hear that satisfying crunch of his jaw breaking, I don't regret it.

And now here I sit in county jail, doin' my nine-month stint for assault. Here I sit, just one more statistic, just one more soldier whose alcohol-induced aggression becomes just one more reason for the local news media, the public, *us*, to believe that this war just ain't worth its weight in shit.

Well, here I sit, just one more version… of *them*.

THE COMBAT VETERAN AT HOME

James J. Slattery

Stephen W. (Brick) McInroy served in the Marine Corps during WWII and saw action over the course of his deployment in the Pacific Theater. I remember well the circumstances of his life in Wellsboro Pennsylvania subsequent to war's end. He had not been seriously wounded nor did he boast medals or commendations of any significance. All the same, his time after return could possibly be termed tragically short. His death might be seen as slow suicide.

The last I ever saw him was a sunny day in 1967. His hollow cheeks, and livid complexion seemed overwhelmed by the huge raccoon eyes staring from beneath the receding widow's peak of once red hair. He was dying of tuberculosis resulting from the removal of a cancerous lung. My aunt Clara had died of a massive stroke in 1953, and with her had gone any possibility of meaningful life remaining him.

This is not to say that there were not happy times. Family reunions, nights with shrimp and hot sauce as we watched "Your Hit Parade," and amazing Lionel Train sets which he sold at his store. Most of all though, I remember Sundays at either the VFW or American Legion. The Pennsylvania Blue Laws prohibited the sale of alcohol on Sunday. But not to such organizations as these, and Uncle Brick had keys to each.

I sat with these men, a child of eleven or twelve, and listened to their tales. One of them, Ransom Giroux, had been gassed in World War I and suffered from impaired lung function. Another had scars, another a vacant stare and a sadness he could not recognize, let alone admit. My father, a non-combat veteran, was of their company. For whatever reason, they welcomed his presence. It is from him that I learned the truth of that time. In response to my asking why these heroes never spoke of their time at war, experiences, I was certain, would be both exciting and edifying, he replied, "They were there. They did what they had to do. And have nothing to say." He then added, "When you hear someone bragging about what he did, be certain he is lying. He probably never even fought."

Those men are all dead. In their time, they held jobs, raised families, went to church on Sunday, and paid their taxes. But to a man, they drank too much, found themselves often on the edge of violence, and seemed lost in the world which held them in such high esteem for doing the very things which haunted them until their passing.

May God understand. May the world never forget them.

ABOUT SOLDIER'S HEART

Soldier's Heart is a national non-profit organization based in Troy, New York whose mission is to transform the emotional, moral, and spiritual wounds that often result from war and military service. We help active-duty troops and veterans develop new and honorable warrior identities. We offer genuine homecoming, reintegration, and a path for post-traumatic growth. We also empower and equip families, care providers, individuals, and communities to support our troops and veterans as they work to establish new identities.

ABOUT THE AUTHOR/EDITOR

John R. Ostwald is a Professor Emeritus (Psychology), newspaper columnist and Viet Nam era veteran of the United States Navy (Inshore Undersea Warfare Group II). His work has been presented at national conferences, and on radio and television.

CPSIA information can be obtained
at www.ICGtesting.com
Printed in the USA
BVOW10s2136130517
484080BV00001B/2/P

9 780692 843895